PAPER FACES

PAPER FACES

by
MICHAEL GRATER

Illustrated by the Author

Photographs by
GEOFFREY GOODE

MILLS & BOON LIMITED
50 Grafton Way, Fitzroy Square,
London W.1.

FIRST PUBLISHED 1967
© *Michael Grater 1967*

By the same Author:
MAKE IT IN PAPER
ONE PIECE OF PAPER

Made and printed by offset in Great Britain
by William Clowes and Sons Ltd
London and Beccles

CONTENTS

INTRODUCTION

Most of us like to make things. When we take some material in our hands and fashion it to create something which was not there before, we can often find a personal satisfaction and pleasure. There are many things we can make, from pictures which require little special equipment to elaborate models which have to be planned and developed with attention to all sorts of detail.

The choice of project we undertake will obviously depend on many factors; where we live, how much we can afford, what interests us, what we have learned, how old we are or how strong, whether we can use tools, the sort of place we have in which to work. If we are young our parents and teachers might help us, and sometimes we will prefer to get on by ourselves. Sometimes, when we are interested, we might manage best without any sort of outside help, and sometimes we will reach the stage when we cannot make any more progress without the help of someone more able or experienced than ourselves. There are many problems involved when we start to make something, but most of these can be solved eventually because there is usually someone who is able to help with the right sort of suggestion or idea.

From the earliest times people have made things, either because they needed them, or for less practical reasons — perhaps because they had time to spare and they became interested in something, interested enough to want to make it in their own way.

Any history of man could have a large section devoted to the things he has made, from the simplest household pot to the great achievements in building and engineering. Making masks and faces is not likely to be included as one of man's greatest achievements, nor is it likely to be an activity which would figure largely in such a history. But men have always made masks. They have looked at their own and at other faces, or they have looked at animals, and they have taken various materials and have recreated in their own way what they have seen.

It is a complicated study to investigate the reasons why men have made masks. They have made them as objects of religion, as images which could be worshipped. They have made them to decorate sacred places, in homage to something or out of fear. Sometimes they have made them to convey a message, and sometimes they have made them to wear in order to change themselves and assume different personalities.

The Latin word *persona*, from which we get the word personality, was the name for the mask worn by the characters in a play, and people have made and worn masks in order to change their own appearance and personality for a variety of reasons. Masks have been made and worn in order to disguise and frighten. They have been used on sad or unpleasant occasions, when warriors or raiding parties wore masks with frightening decorations in order to terrify. And they have been used on happy occasions at carnivals and parties. We are fortunate today in having come a long way from the time when men made masks in order to terrify other men. Today we would only make masks for fun or amusement, or to wear as a disguise for plays and public shows.

When we sit in front of a mirror it is difficult to resist making faces at ourselves. We poke out our tongue, or pull the flesh down to change and distort the shape of our eyes. We push our nose up at the tip or flatten it against our face. We do this probably because we know the familiar image of our own face and we are intrigued to see what we might have been, or what we could perhaps become. It is an interesting thing to stand in front of a mirror and to try to change one's appearance in order to see an apparent personality change. If we study the effects of facial movement closely we find it possible to communicate a variety of reactions or ideas. We can screw our face up into a tight grimace of dislike or even of revulsion. We can take an idea and see how we can change our face to suit the idea. How would we look, for example, if we were poor and very hungry? We can see this perhaps by making our cheeks hollow, by sucking in and by tightening our mouths to appear sad.

Some of us will do this sort of solo performance in front of mirrors — not all the time of course — because it gives us a secret amusement. Our faces are funny. We can do extraordinary things with them because they are a complexity of muscles and changing shapes. When we think of all the people in different parts of the world who make funny faces in front of mirrors we have to smile at the ridiculous spectacle presented. So why, if we can stand in front of mirrors, should we make masks? Firstly, we can make them to extend the fun — for our own pleasure and also to amuse others. We can make interesting and amusing shapes, and we can wear them. We can also discover and enjoy ways of decorating and making them attractive with colours and pattern.

If we can make the masks visually attractive, so that people will enjoy looking at them, we can use them for decorations, either for parties and special occasions, or merely because we like to have colourful and exciting things around us.

Sometimes we might make a mask for a special occasion, for a play, or for a show put on by the school or by an organisation we belong to.

When you stand in front of a mirror you will see that there are many ways of making faces. There are also many ways of making masks. The work illustrated in this book is for people who like to make things. A method is suggested and developed for working with simple and readily available materials. The end product of all the exercises will be a mask or a head, and most of these can be made in paper. A few of the later more elaborate exercises will work best in thin card, but all of them are possible without any great expense or searching for equipment and materials.

The exercises suggested are a type of sculpture in paper, in which forms or shapes are raised by cutting and folding deliberately, making the paper do exactly what you intend it to. If you take a sheet of wrapping paper and try to stand it on its edge it will fall flat as many times as you try to make it stand. But if you make a fold down the centre of the paper so that there are two surfaces or planes, the paper will probably support itself, and instead of dropping flat, will stand upright. If you take the same sheet of paper and make it into a simple open-ended cylinder, pinning or clipping it at the seam, it will again stand on end unsupported. In both cases you have been deliberately controlling the material by using simple modelling techniques.

The examples described in this book are planned in a simple developing order so that anyone attempting them can expect to develop an ability to control and manipulate paper and card. At the same time he will be able to establish a vocabulary of simple techniques on which to base more advanced work later.

The first exercise requires only the slightest technical ability, no more in fact than the ability to fold the paper and to make simple cuts with a pair of scissors, establishing in the first mask a place for the nose, and cut-out eyes for the wearer to see through.

From this point, if you are interested enough to continue the exercises, you will make a series of masks with slight developments which systematically illustrate some of the possibilities of the material.

There are accompanying suggestions for papers and cards, and for ideas and sources of pattern and decoration. Later exercises illustrating specific animal shapes can be attempted for fun, or they can be made deliberately by teachers or anyone concerned with the production of a play in which the shape might be used. The examples suggested are basic shapes which can be treated in a variety of ways to make them either useful or decorative. Suggestions are also made in the text for methods of making the paper or card masks more durable.

The material used in any of the work suggested need not be expensive sheets of paper. If you are interested enough and able to buy paper or sheets of card you will have the advantage of starting with the best materials. But if you are unable to buy the material, much of it can be salvaged from cartons and wrapping paper. This can be painted or decorated in various ways during the process of making the masks, and for this purpose you should aim to have access to paints and pastes. Scraps of coloured material collected from various sources will prove useful to paste on to the masks in some exercises. For longer usage some of the suggested shapes can be made up in card and used as a foundation for layers of sized or stiffened canvas or hessian. References to potential methods and to treatments are made throughout the text, but in the beginning the first exercises can be attempted with a minimum of equipment.

You will require only some paper and paints or crayons, a little string, some paste and a pair of scissors. With this equipment and a place to work, if you are a child or if you are an adult, if you have a little experience or none at all, as long as you are interested you can go from this point of introduction straight into the practical craft of paper faces.

THE MASK

The simplest of all masks is the rectangular piece of paper folded at the centre, from which holes are cut for eyes, and from which an inverted V-shape is cut so that the nostrils and mouth are not covered. You should begin your work on mask-making by cutting and wearing this shape now, so that within a few minutes of starting your practical experiments you are actually sitting with a mask on—like an old-time highwayman. A section of the mask cut away at the sides will form a projection which can be the point of fastening. By taking a little care at this stage you should find it possible to rest the mask on the tops of your ears. In order that you may wear the mask it is necessary to make fixtures on both sides. Holes can be made in the projecting pieces above the ears with a paper or leather punch, or with a spike of some sort—a bradawl or even a sharp nail can be used for this. These holes can be the fixture points for strings which can be tied at the back of the head, or for rubber bands which can be threaded through their own loops and stretched over the ears.

Since there is inevitably at this point a strain on the mask which is likely to tear the paper before it has had much use, the fixture should be strengthened in some way. This can be done either by sticking pieces of paper behind the holes, or by folding the paper double at each of the sides before piercing the holes. In cutting the mask it is obviously necessary to take care to position the holes for the eyes so that they can be seen through when it is worn. To do this the paper should be held in front of the face with the fold at the centre, and a pencil mark should be made at the exact point of the eye on one side. Holes for the eyes can be cut round as in the diagram (Fig. 1), or if this is found to be difficult, they can be cut in an easier shape. Triangles or squares are easier to cut for example, than circles—although the circles are visually more satisfying. With a little practice you should be able to find a way of cutting them so that the edges are not too ragged.

Suitable papers for this type of mask can be found almost anywhere. They can be bought, in which case good quality drawing paper is the best to use—coloured if it is available. Or they can be found around the house. A fairly stiff used envelope can be cut to make a very satisfactory mask, and wrapping paper is even better. Brown wrapping paper can be collected in a variety of different tones and thicknesses. It is

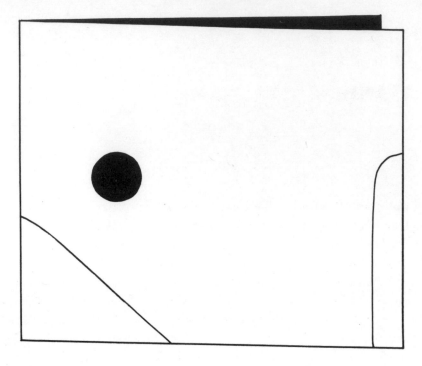

Fig. 1

usually thrown away after the parcel has been unwrapped and it is excellent for mask-making.

Cardboard cartons are a further useful source of material. The rectangles for this exercise can be cut from cereal cartons or from other salvaged materials. Corrugated paper or card is good for a stiff hard-wearing type of mask and has the further advantage of being interesting to look at. These and other materials which you can search out for yourself are available in almost every home, and have the considerable attraction of not costing anything.

DEVELOPING THE MASK

Edge Cutting

The simple folded and cut mask will present no difficulties to anyone. As long as it can be worn without its falling down over the wearer's eyes it is successful, and can now be developed with added interest.

The simple shape can be made visually interesting by cutting the edges in a pattern (Fig. 2). This can be done symmetrically with the paper folded, or if card is used it can be done by cutting through one thickness with the mask out flat. It is almost certain that the first time the edge is cut the person making the mask will cut a simple saw edge by snipping out V-shapes from the original. This is in no way wrong, but there

Fig. 2 — The simple mask shape can be developed by cutting the edges into a pattern.

Fig. 3

are many variations on this kind of cut, and investigations at this stage of different types of edge-cutting will prove useful in later exercises.

Attempts at simple variations of the cut will result in two things: the cutter will improve his ability to manipulate paper and scissors and will, through seeing and comparing the results, add to his knowledge and awareness of what is visually and artistically effective in paper. Small intricate cuts, for example, seen from a distance will appear less effective than those produced by a simple and bold treatment.

A certain amount of experimental cutting can be tried merely by sitting down with the paper and scissors, but the exercises might be made more rewarding and interesting if the maker relies less on luck and accident but goes out of his way to look for ideas to use. A close look at the edges of various leaves might suggest new shapes to explore.

The edge of a seaweed or a pattern of clouds in the sky might suggest an idea for further experiment (Fig. 3). There is no reason why the edge shape should not be drawn before the mask is cut, so that the maker can have some idea, before cutting, of the effect he will produce.

Even at this early stage it is possible to add to one's knowledge of what happens to paper when it is treated in certain ways. Strips of paper, although cut straight in the first instance, can be made to curl by running a sharp edge along one surface. This technique can be learned by anyone to whom it is new by taking a thin strip of paper, the width of a ruler is a suitable width to begin with, and holding one end between the fingers. Beginning at the point where the strip is held, a knife or scissor blade held in the other hand is drawn along the under surface of the paper, between the sharp edge of the blade and the thumb. This scraping action will break the tension on one surface and the paper will spring into a neat curl. The tendency at first is naturally to be too gentle so that the surface is hardly scraped enough, or to pull so hard that the strip is torn at the point where it is held. Difficulty with the technique can be overcome with patience and practice, and the skill can very quickly become firmly established in the vocabulary of the person experimenting. A mask with curly edges can be visually exciting, but it must be remembered that this is a technique for use with paper only. It cannot be done effectively with anything but paper and the very thinnest card.

Variable and interesting edges of the masks discovered in this exercise can be compared for visual effect. They should all be interesting to look at but particular treatment might make some appear more effective than others. The important factor in discovering the shapes is the use to which they might be put in the future, when you will really be concerned with making masks which are attractive and impressive both in shape and decoration.

Painting and Decorating

The cut mask can be made visually more effective by a patterned or decorative treatment of the surface.

Drawn or Painted Pattern

Patterns on the surface of masks can be drawn or painted. They can be put on with coloured pencils or crayons, with dyes or inks, or with any interesting colouring materials or methods which are available. Any mask can be used as an experimental surface for work with colours and textures.

An ink blot made deliberately in the centre fold of a mask can be developed into an interesting visual pattern if the paper is folded in half on the wet blot. A first blot can be left to dry, or other blots can be made over the top of it in order to develop the

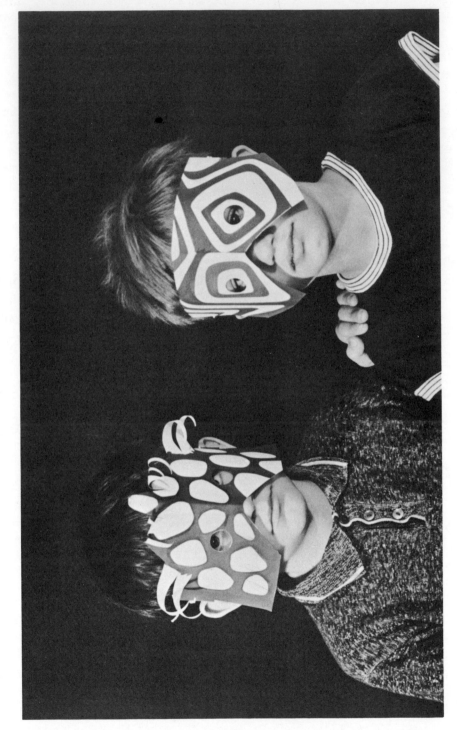

Fig. 4—The mask can be made visually interesting with pattern or decorative treatment.

pattern. The dry blot can be used as a starting point on which to develop further drawn or painted shapes with a pen or with a brush.

As an experiment the mask can be finger painted all over. This is a technique which will give an interesting surface effect and texture to the mask, because the pigment can be made smoother or rougher by using the finger or finger nail in a variety of different ways to spread the paint.

For a simple and immediate effect a mask cut in plain white paper can be painted one colour all over and can be allowed to dry before other pattern is added. You can learn a great deal about colour by making deliberate experiments. For example a mask painted all over red can be effective enough to be worn without further treatment. It can, however, be treated in a number of ways in order to give it more appeal.

The red mask can have a patterned treatment in completely different colours. It can be painted in greens and yellows and blues and any other colours you like to mix. Or it can have pattern in different tones or shades of the same colour. We cannot really know what is the difference between the treatments until we have done the work and can make a comparison by looking at the masks and seeing the finished effects.

As a preliminary exercise in making a visual effect you could learn from making a set number of masks with different pattern treatment. You could cut for this experiment three identical masks. The first of these should be decorated in any way you like, using any colours and shapes which occur to you as you work. As you work you should notice that you will stop occasionally and hold the mask away from you at arm's length in order to see the effect you are creating. You might even occasionally put the mask on and get up to look in a mirror.

The second mask could be painted all over in one colour, and when it is dry you could try mixing new tones of the background colour, and painting your pattern with these only. For example, a yellow mask will have its pattern and decoration in other yellows. If you are using paints you will find these yellows by mixing the original colour in different proportions with white or with black. If you are using crayons it is not quite so simple, but different tones can be found by drawing one colour over another.

The third mask can be painted all over in the same colour as the second, but can have its pattern in black and white only. The white can be painted on after the background has dried or, if you plan it in the early stages and are working on a white background, the ground colour can be incorporated into the actual pattern. After completing an exercise like this you will have a number of things which you can compare. In this instance you will have three masks with different treatments. It is not necessary to try to guess which will be better than the others. You will have them in front of you to look at and compare. If you look carefully you will begin to appreciate in a simple way the visual effects of the different treatments.

The first one with random colouring might be quite exciting. It will depend on

2

what sort of colours you have selected and used. But it might be less easy to look at than the second one, in which the range of colours is much closer together and easier to take in at a glance.

The second mask is likely to be rather more gentle than the third, in which the extreme contrast between the colour and the black and white is likely to make a visual bang. If you want a mask which has an immediate and startling impact you should be able to see by comparing these three examples which is likely to prove most effective. And if you want a more pleasing and attractive effect you should also be able to see a suitable treatment. If you want to learn about colour, and if you are keen to know something about the visual effects of different treatments, you must experiment deliber-ately, so that you can see and compare the results. By comparing you will learn to recognise what is effective, and will be able to choose the best combinations of colour and tone in later exercises.

You can at this early stage take one colour and you can benefit enormously by working at it in a systematic and orderly way. Most people will answer when asked to name their favourite colour, and it will usually be a single word answer. But any one colour has a large range of visual potential and difference. It can be light or dark in many different degrees, and with certain treatments it can begin to change in many subtle and exciting ways, gradually losing its original effect as it begins to change into a different colour.

If you are interested enough to want to find out about colours and the way they change, you could take your favourite colour, and using black or white, you could alter it into as many tones as possible. You could paint a whole mask in different stripes of the same colour, or you could start circles at the eyes and paint outwards, gradually changing the tones. This will teach you a great deal about your favourite colour.

You will learn even more if you take the same colour and mix it with a different colour. If you are really interested you can begin with the primary colours, red, blue and yellow, and will find out in the first place what happens when you mix them, and secondly what happens when you use the results.

You will never, of course, know all there is to know about colour, but if you use the masks as simple shapes on which to experiment you will find interesting results emerging from your colour-mixing exercises. And you will gradually build up an ability to select and use a suitable decoration on the masks you will make on later occasions. This ability will be valuable to you, not only in the mask-making activity, but also in general. It will help you to choose when you are faced with the need to make a selection between various colours—when you are buying things to wear, or choosing presents for people. You will be able to understand what other people have done with colours—when you go to the theatre or when you sit in a restaurant. Someone is always using colour somewhere. It is all around us wherever we are, in the city, where it is mostly man-made, or in the country where it is mostly natural and often even more exciting.

Sometimes, as you experiment and learn about colour and pattern, the masks on which you have worked will be messy and dirty. They will be streaked with paint where you have not been able to control it, and there will be muddy effects where you wanted bright colours. You must make mistakes, and you must accept this fact. If the result of any exercise is not as pleasing as you intended, then you must throw the mask away and start again. The experience will not be a costly one, and if you have learned from the mistakes, you will be that much more able as a craftsman in your future work.

Cut Paper Decoration

Painting is sometimes inconvenient, and sometimes in your work—although you might enjoy cutting the masks—you might not feel inclined to paint. There are other methods of decoration, and one which can be particularly effective is that in which the mask is treated with a collage of added paper.

Cut or torn paper stuck to the mask can produce interesting visual and surface results. A useful and never-ending source of coloured paper can be found in old magazines. This paper, torn or cut out and pasted to the mask, will give a quite different effect from painting. The surface will be more textured, and the mask itself will become thicker with the added paper. Interesting visual results can be achieved by actually building on the surface of the mask with stuck paper, making a suggestion of form—for example at the eyebrows or on the end of the nose.

Interesting patterns and designs can be discovered by cutting different shapes and colours and sticking them over others. It is exciting to see how many tones of one colour can be found from the illustrations and advertisements in one magazine alone.

A brown paper mask can be effectively decorated with a pattern cut from different brown papers. If a little time and care is spent collecting the wrappings from parcels it is astonishing how many different types of the one colour are to be found in something as simple as brown wrapping paper. Tissue paper is available now in a wide range of very exciting colours and tones. Pasted on a mask, especially over previously painted decoration, the tissue will give an interesting textured surface. Used on its own against a plain background it will produce a beautiful range of subtle and exciting colour effects where one coloured tissue overlaps another.

Other interesting effects in paper collage might be found by experiment. Postage stamps are an excellent source of colour and tone. They are easy to collect and can be stuck on to make various deliberate patterns.

For general use almost any paste or adhesive will be found suitable. A further advantage of the stuck decoration is that it tends to make the mask stiffer and stronger than the original material.

Sources of Pattern

In many of the exercises you will discover things about colour by decorating all or part of the mask. You might find that the colour you used to think of as red is only one of a whole range of tones from darkest red to pink. If you set out deliberately to mix colours you will find yourself suddenly making particular colours, like the red of a certain type of car or like the red of a tomato or some other fruit. When we get into a car or eat a tomato we probably do not really look at the colour. Most of the time we take colour for granted, and when it comes to using it we are often rather lazy about it. This is a pity since colours can be exciting, especially when they are put together by someone who is looking for new and interesting effects.

Anyone mixing colours will make mistakes. Colours can begin by being very bright and clean, but mixed in the wrong way they can easily become muddy and dirty. This will often result from haphazard mixing in which there is no deliberate aim.

If you cut a simple mask shape and start to work on the surface in colour you will find it quite easy to make some sort of pattern. Some people will paint with small or gentle brush strokes, watching the effect they are making and trying desperately to do the right thing. Others will dab new colour onto the surface as though they are in a hurry to get the job finished.

Some people will paint wandering and free lines and fill in the spaces they make, and others will work carefully, building the pattern with order and in a sequence which pleases them.

There are no firm rules about making patterns, although we can sometimes find factors which might help the process. It is, for example, not always the best thing to rely on luck or accident. If, when you are painting a pattern, you allow the brush to wander about uncertainly over the surface you might find something interesting. You might also find something which turns out to be a lot less attractive than you really intended. If this occurs too frequently you might begin to consider the process, and look for ways of developing a firmer ability to work with colours and pattern towards a more satisfying and successful end product.

In the first place you will need to extend the range of your work so that you have an increased variety in the combinations of shape and colour which you are able to use. You can do this gradually by going out of your way to look at things in order to discover what sort of patterns they have, or what sort of patterns they make. If you look for patterns in the world around you, you will find an enormous storehouse of suggestions for colour and shape experiments which you might adapt and use for your own purpose. The most rewarding source of pattern discovery is clearly the world of nature. It does not matter where you live, from the room in which you are working, across the land to the seashore — and even beyond, there is always something natural that is worth looking at.

A leaf held in the hand has its own mysterious arrangement of colours and shapes. If you take these colours and shapes and remake them in your own way on a different surface, enlarging them as much as you like, you will create a decorative treatment which will only exist because you held the leaf in your hand and looked at it. The pattern which results from this leaf will not be the result of luck or accident. It will have been developed from deliberate observation, and because you took the trouble when looking to select and to recreate. It is unlikely that your own version of the pattern will be anything like exact in colours and shapes, but this is not important. The important thing is to find a pattern different from the one you might have found by dabbing at random and with no real planning.

The pattern which you find must not, of course, be a picture of the leaf. This is a different thing, and not what you are concerned with in looking for a way of assisting your work with masks. It has to be an arrangement of colours and shapes, adjusted and adapted to cover the surface you are working on, and it need not be in any way recognisable as an associate part of the object from which it was evolved.

If you can find an interesting pattern development by looking at a leaf, there is an unlimited range of further pattern opportunity for you to discover without the need to make any great effort. Other leaves have different tones and visual arrangements. Flowers are worth examining closely. They often have beautifully subtle arrangements of tones and shapes in the centre part where they are not normally subjected to very close examination.

Fruit and vegetables will provide a very accessible source of pattern, especially if they are looked at in new ways, if, for example, they are cut in half so that you can see the way they grow outwards from the centre.

If you live near the seashore there are again never-ending sources of patterns and surfaces to be explored. Pebbles and shells are particularly fine to hold and to observe. The way a shell grows is visually interesting, with subtle but very strong and firm lines. A bone washed up on the beach, or a piece of cork or timber can suggest a type of pattern.

If you are unable to go to a beach to look for natural objects to use as sources of pattern, you might be able to go to a wood where there are other objects. The barks of trees are interesting, fungi, mosses and pieces of broken or rotting branch are everywhere in the woods, and can be picked up and used as points of departure for pattern making. The pattern can be as freely developed as you like to make it. In any exercises, it does not matter from what source you are working, the intention is to make a personal experiment and to assist yourself in the process of finding ways to arrange colours and shapes.

Like any other man-made object a mask can have any sort of pattern treatment (Fig. 5). The shapes which form the basis of the pattern can be developed from your observation of natural objects, or they can be developed from your observation of other types of object.

You might sit at your work table and see ideas for pattern simply by looking around you. Cracks in the ceiling, an arrangement of objects on a shelf, pieces of paper cut out and dropped on the floor as you were working can suggest shapes which will start you on the pattern process.

You might find an interesting pattern by taking a simple geometric shape and developing it in your own way. A circle drawn round a convenient object, such as a glass tumbler, can be manipulated in many ways to make a pattern. It can be overlapped with other circles to produce areas suitable for colouring. It can be used to make the visual effect of a chain, or it can be built up growing from the centre, like something seen under a microscope and enlarged.

It can be combined with part circles or with other geometric shapes. A circle can have a square inside it, or a triangle. It can be placed around other squares or arranged with other triangles, and the patterns can be developed to grow in any required direction—upwards and downwards for example, like something bouncing. There are many possible arrangements of simple geometric shapes in which the actual shapes, although made separately, will combine in the end product to make patterns all over the surface being decorated. These patterns are interesting to find but you must remember that the more precise the shapes are, and the more complicated they get, the more difficult it will be to paint them because of the sharp edges. This is an example of the type of work in which cut paper patterns would be easier to apply than a painted decoration. A simple pattern of stripes can be effective because the contrast between the colours used is direct and uncomplicated. We can take in the effect at a glance, without having to work hard to sort something out and arrange it into an acceptable order. In some instances a striped pattern can be given additional interest by the introduction of very simple variations. The thickness of the stripes can be varied, for example, by contrasting thin with thick as a regular striped pattern contrasts dark with light, or one colour with another.

When you are working in some of the exercises the type of pattern likely to be most suitable will sometimes be suggested by the shape itself. A tiger mask will suggest a pattern of stripes in yellow and black, which is an arrangement of colours having an immediate appeal, and some of the bird shapes will probably look best with a pattern suggesting the arrangement of feathers. But there are shapes suitable for gay and exciting colour experiments, and it will be of enormous value for anyone attempting the masks to rely less on luck as a source of decoration, and to look more for ideas

Fig. 5

in the world around. This process will enlarge any craftsman's ability to decorate his work, and will make the visual world firstly a place which is important to his work, and secondly a place of constant excitement and interest in which to live.

After you have tried and examined various ways of painting patterns on your masks, and as you progress to more advanced work, you will find that there are other points to consider in selecting and putting on a decoration. When you have learned to make an attractive pattern without great difficulty, you will be able to be more deliberate in aiming at a particular effect. If you want something which is merely as attractive as you can make it, then good pattern will be enough, and you will need to do no more than use your eyes in the right way. Masks can, however, be used to communicate rather more than a simple pattern and colour appeal. They can be made to suggest an idea. The most obvious example of this is the plain black mask worn to disguise the wearer at the same time as it conveys a simple and sinister message. If someone wearing a black mask were to burst into a room where you were sitting quietly, the probable immediate effect would be one of concern and alarm. This would not be so, of course, if you recognised your small brother under the mask, but if the situation were real, you would probably be right in anticipating some sort of unpleasant intention on the part of the wearer of the black mask.

If, on the other hand, the figure burst in wearing a black mask with orange and yellow stripes you would probably be less concerned. The effect of the masks would be quite different. The coloured one would attract your attention to the wearer, but it would not convey the same impression of nastiness. When you decorate a mask you can consider the effect you are going to create, and you can choose a pattern and colour style to achieve this effect. A deep purple mask with black edges and grey lines round the eyes is obviously not the sort of thing to wear at a party, or in a play where you need to establish a light-hearted character. If you want an amusing mask you must use bright colours and pleasing shapes. You can find suggestions for shapes and their arrangement by looking around you, and you will find that there are always plenty of ideas to use as a source of decoration. But when you want to communicate a particular effect with a mask you must select and choose with special care.

In the main, therefore, there are two things to consider in putting colour and pattern on a mask. Firstly, you should try to find a pattern which is visually attractive and which, as you work with it, will help you to discover a little more than you already know about colours and shapes. Secondly, you must try to make sure that the pattern is right for the idea you want to communicate. Is the mask gay or cheerful? Or is it a frightening thing to be seen in? Both types of work are possible, and both are valid.

After investigating and understanding the range of possibilities of the simpler mask shapes, you can begin to learn more skill in the craft by attempting some of the developments in the following exercises. It is not necessary, unless you want to, to attempt every exercise. But as you go on to another mask shape you should read the various suggestions, so that you do not miss something of potential importance in technique and skill.

The Mask Cut with a Nose

The diagram (Fig. 6) illustrates a simple method of incorporating a nose shape into the mask. If the mask is cut double on a centre fold, indicated in this and subsequent diagrams by the vertical line at the left of the diagram — or by the filled-in shape at the top which points to the fold, the shape can be folded downwards so that when the mask is open it projects forward like a nose in the centre (Fig. 7).

Since the mask is cut double on a centre fold the direction of the fold on the actual nose must be reversed when the nose is folded into position. It is necessary, when you cut the nose, to remember that if it is cut too wide it will cover the eye holes when it is folded down, and it will not be possible for the wearer to see when he has the mask on. The nose can be deliberately shaped in cutting in order to overcome this minor snag.

Any masks made with the nose incorporated, either in paper or card, can be used as exercises in pattern development, but the real object of this exercise is to learn the

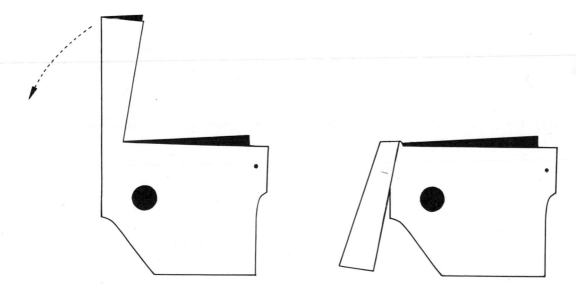

Fig. 6

Fig. 7—The mask can be cut with a nose shape which can be turned down to project at the front.

simple technique of including a nose. When it is included the nose should give a convincing suggestion of form into the original shape of the mask. Like all modelling in paper or card, it should be crisp and uncrumpled, and as simple and uncomplicated as possible in form. There is nothing to be gained from including unnecessary detail since the effect is going to be seen from a distance in most cases, and small fussy details will hardly be noticed.

Clowns

The nose in Fig. 6 is a simple shape, wider at its base than at the top, but it can be cut and developed with many interesting variations of form. In Fig. 8 it is shown cut large and bulbous, like the noses worn by circus clowns. The mask on the left in the photograph is the simple shape. In the middle the same shape has been cut with large eyebrows. This part of the paper has been cut from the original in the first example, but has been included in the second — firstly to avoid unnecessary waste, and secondly so that it can be made visually effective by cutting it into simple points.

The mask shown on the right includes a simple chin and mouth shape. This inclusion makes the original cut slightly more complicated and is illustrated in the diagram, Fig. 9.

Fig. 8—The nose can be made into a definite shape, like the bulbous noses worn by clowns.

Fig. 9

To read this diagram, and any others in the book, it is only necessary to look closely at it and to understand what it really says. You will probably not be able to do this at first glance, and you will have to study the diagram so that you can work it out in your own way, assisted by reference to the relevant descriptions in the text.

In this instance the paper is obviously intended to be folded at the centre, the fold being as usual on the left side. The nose, which is to be bent downwards (Fig. 6), is indicated at the top of the shape, and the eyebrow cuts are suggested in that part of the paper which might otherwise have been cut away. The hole for the eye is indicated by the black circle. The cut in the approximate centre of the face will allow the mask to be placed over the nose without any discomfort to the wearer. The chin and cheek forms are indicated in the shape at the bottom, open side of the mask. This shape is simple and direct because the mask is a simple version styled on the appearance of the traditional clown. It is not meant to be real, but rather to communicate in an instant the idea intended, and for this reason it is simplified to immediate essentials. There is a minimum of modelling because if you attempt the mask you will not be trying to produce something which is a disguise that no one can see through. You should be aiming for a simple and immediate impact, and it is again necessary to avoid unnecessary complications which, although they may be difficult to do properly, will add nothing to the end result.

Clown masks can be varied (Fig. 10). You could make a whole range of them if you liked for a party. Some could be fat and some thin—some could have long hair, which you could curl, and some could have straight hair sticking out at the sides. Decorating the clown masks could be exciting, almost like making up your own face like a clown, which is something a lot of us would probably quite like to do.

As a further development of this mask the clowns could be cut, still on a centre fold, to incorporate a simple and large bow-tie under the chin. These could be painted in bright colours with attractive pattern, and they could be made a suitable size for wearing.

They could also be drawn and cut larger than life-size, and could be used as decorations for a party or for Christmas. If, after painting, they are pinned to the wall partly folded so that the masks project forward slightly, they will be visually interesting because the two sides of the fold will be different in tone according to the source of light in the room. The fold will furthermore strengthen the masks as decorations, so that they can be expected to remain in position without sagging. The brightly coloured ties can be allowed to flop or curl into their own shapes, or they can be pinned in a permanent and pleasing position when the decorations are put up.

It is amusing after a party where you have had clown decorations to give each of your guests a mask to take home as a souvenir. It is better still to have materials ready when they arrive, and to let them make their own masks to decorate at the party and to take home for themselves when it is over. It is only necessary for you to organise the materials, and to have scissors and paper ready—and for you to show them how to set about doing it.

Fig. 10—When the shape is understood it can be varied in size and proportion to give visually different effects to one idea.

People

People are interesting in many different ways. When we know them and talk to them we can usually find something that appeals to us, or that will attract our attention to them. Or we might find something which we do not like about them. Everyone is interesting in some way. And the ones we do not know can be very interesting to look at.

We see people everywhere—in the streets and in the shops, in schools and on buses—and they are all different to look at. There are the tall ones with thin faces and dark eyes, the ones with lined faces, and the ones with sharp cheek bones. There are the ones we find attractive, and others we might consider ugly—hairy ones and smooth ones. And we could go on listing them for many pages. Any of these, and any other type of person, can be used as a basis for a simple mask shape. In masks any human style is possible (Fig. 11). The shapes can be observed anywhere and drawn before cutting, but after drawing you should see if it is possible to simplify your shapes so that the cutting stage will not be too involved.

In every case you should be able to cut the mask on the fold, with the nose included, as before, at the top of the forehead, so that it can be turned down afterwards to give form at the front. Hair and whiskers can be curled where they are included, to give more form and interest, and the masks can obviously be coloured. There are as many different shapes possible as there are different people.

It is rude to stare at people, although you must obviously look at them when you are travelling in the same bus or train, or are waiting in the same place. But if you look as closely as you are able, without causing offence to anyone, you will find almost anywhere you go a useful storehouse for more suggestions and ideas for masks you might make. You will see so many different types of people when you really start looking, with different profiles and different expressions, that you will come to realise in fact that the small part of the world in which you live is full of a great variety of people.

When you are setting out to study faces you should try to discover real points of difference between people. You should try to notice the shape of the face; what happens to the chin—does it jut forward, is it round and comfortable or is it a small, neat shape? Noses are interesting. They can be seen in all sorts of shapes and sizes, and can be used in simplified versions to make your masks interesting. Hair is obviously a useful feature to include in masks. It can be on the top of the head, or on the eyebrows or chin, and it can be usefully included in a simple mask as a moustache. The moustache is not as popular today as it used to be, but it is a very easy shape to incorporate. It can be large and simple and black (Fig. 12), and can be effectively cut so that it covers most of the lower part of the face. Moustaches can droop, or they can be

Fig. 11

Fig. 12—Different types of people can be portrayed in simple masks. A moustache or beard will contrast effectively with the plain shape of the mask.

made to curl. They can appear to grow upwards or downwards, and will make an immediate visual impact in the mask.

Beards in various styles are also easy to incorporate into a cut mask and, like hair, they can be curled into patterns which will make interesting contrasts with the plainer surfaces of the mask itself. Different-shaped mouths are interesting to try. The mouth turned up at the sides, which smiles, is well known because it contrasts easily with its opposite which turns down and is glum. A round mouth, or one with teeth cut and protruding will present a different appearance. You will find that variations on the usual mouth shape will change the whole expression of the mask.

After attempting a range of interesting human masks which can be worn, it might be interesting to make a series of decorative masks based on human forms. These can be made and put together into a simple totem pole. They could be mounted above each other on a door, or on the side of a cupboard or wardrobe.

To make a really effective decoration the colour factor could in some way be organised and deliberate. This would only be necessary where the totem pole was going to be on public view, perhaps on a social occasion at school or at a club, and there are too many possible types of colour arrangement to list. If you are unable to

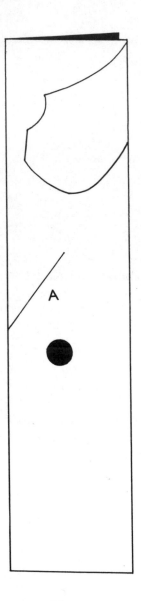

Fig. 13

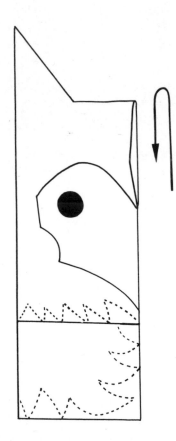

Fig. 14

get started on a suitable arrangement you might paint each mask one colour only, with the pattern on each in black and white. Or each mask could be painted with one side one colour, and the other side in a different colour. In this case the pattern on each side could repeat the colour on the other.

It is generally good visually to organise the pattern and colour in a decoration so that there is somewhere a simple formula. This will be a guide for you in making the decoration. The simplest formula is to have the decoration in one colour, varying the tones wherever possible to make it pleasing. But although this can be very good it is rather unadventurous, and the results are always rather as one would expect. The factor of the sudden surprise effect which can come sometimes in colour work, and which can make the decoration unexpectedly exciting, is not likely to occur when you use only one colour.

Both types of colour work are right, and one is certainly not better than the other. What is necessary is to commit yourself to a formula, deciding on what effect you want and what you are going to do. This formula will tell you at each stage of the work what you should do next. It will also make the work of anyone looking at the totem pole easier, because they will be aware at a glance that there is repetition and something familiar running throughout the scheme.

With human masks we can sometimes create characters which are immediately recognisable. This is a simple form of portraiture, but it can only be attempted when the person to be portrayed has simple and easily identified characteristics.

A variation on the simple mask for use at Christmas can be cut (Fig. 13) with the nose and moustache at the top on the original fold. A cut made obliquely into the fold above the eye (A) will allow the top half of the mask to be folded downwards over the front (Fig. 14). A little trimming, as in the dotted lines, will shape the moustache and beard to create the simple Father Christmas mask (Fig. 15). This can be further decorated with appropriate colour, and can either be worn (Fig. 16), or be made in various sizes for a Christmas decoration.

Decorations for parties and special occasions can be made almost as easily as they can be bought. Father Christmas shapes, made like this mask but varied in proportions between fat and thin, could be mingled with some of the clowns suggested earlier. When they are made in paper they are so light that they can be fixed to the wall with ordinary dressmaker's pins, which do negligible damage if they are fixed in the first place with some care. When they are pinned to the wall the masks which are cut symmetrically from folded paper can be allowed to project forward because, as you have already seen, the fold will strengthen the original paper.

A different sort of decoration can be developed by fixing two masks back to back. This can again be done with pins, and the shape made by the two masks can be hung with a cotton pinned to the ceiling. In this case the decoration made from the two masks will turn slowly, and if the expressions are different on the faces the visual

Fig. 15

effect should be quite interesting. If for any reason it is not possible to pin the cottons of the combined masks directly into the ceiling, thin strings can be stretched across the room and the paper masks hung from them. The range of human masks can be made to include any particular face you want. For Hallowe'en parties a collection of witches with long noses and straggling hair will add to the atmosphere. These could have faces in different tones of green, and to make things gay you could include simple ears in the masks, and could make up brightly coloured earrings for them to wear.

For an unusual party you could make totem poles as wall decorations, and could present each guest on arrival with a simple Indian mask with feathers cut from card and patterned. If your parties are wild enough you could make vivid tribal masks, like the primitive ones which are only to be found now in museums. These could be

Fig. 16—Faces with obvious characteristics are easy to establish in masks and are immediately recognisable.

glaring and showing their teeth at the guests, and to add to the fun you could have them in odd places in the house.

People's faces are always interesting. You will be more aware of this by now if you have made a number of masks, and by looking hard when you go out in future you will almost certainly find other faces with particular and perhaps unusual characteristics which you will wish to include in another mask. There are, however, many other sorts of faces and masks for you to experiment on.

Simple Animal Masks

After trying a number of human shapes as a point of departure for mask-making, you can look at animals for a range of new ideas. When we really trouble to observe animals we can often be surprised by their similarity to humans. If you take a mask shape and include a large ear at the flat top (Fig. 17) you are almost able to span the gap between animal and human. When you turn the nose downwards and open the mask you will have a simple cat-like shape (Fig. 18). This should be fairly easy to identify, but the only real difference between this and the human mask is the large ears. It helps, as you will see if you look closely at the diagrams, to cut a characteristic shape at the bottom of the mask, so that the suggestion of cat-like cheeks is established. This is a further example of the sort of simple and immediate treatment you must aim to get into your work. It illustrates the way the right shape works, whereas any amount of unnecessary trimming and scissor juggling might add nothing, and will in fact probably detract from the form you want to make.

The cat shapes can be treated as in previous exercises and can be varied in proportion. They can be anything from fat to thin. They can be short and squat or exaggerated into a really long mask. But whatever their shape, you must remember when drawing and cutting them that, if they are to be worn, the holes for eyes must be cut to suit the wearer.

Slots can be cut in the lower cheeks of the cat masks (Fig. 18 A) and can be used as fixture points for added shapes. These can be cut with flaps which will fit the slots, like the whiskers illustrated in the diagram. This is an acceptable method of making

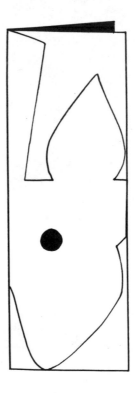

Fig. 17

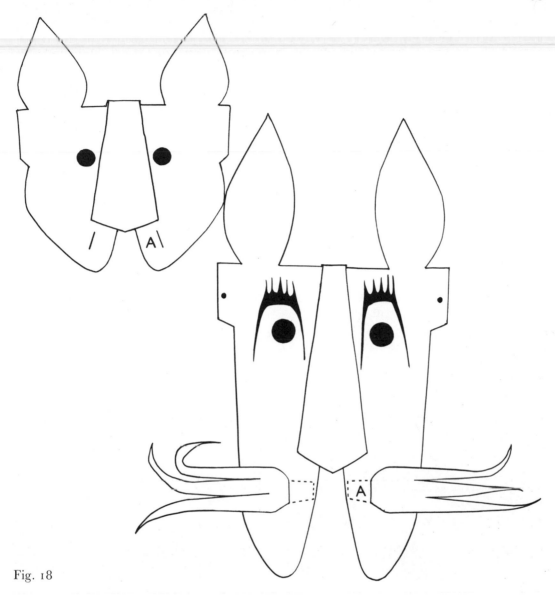

Fig. 18

a fixture when modelling in paper. The shape to be added is cut with flaps in the right place. The flaps can be inserted through the slots in the main surface, and can then be gummed out of sight at the back. This method of fixing has the clear advantage of being neat and almost invisible, and helps the modeller to keep a clean and un-cluttered quality in the finished work. To get the right position for an additional shape, it should be held in place on the surface it is joining, and marks for the slots should be made with a pencil, or better still with the point of a pin. The line between the pin-holes can be cut in exactly the right position when the shape is removed.

Whiskers for a cat mask can stick out sideways, or they can be fixed at an angle so that they droop and curl.

The shapes suggested in the diagram can be a starting point for further experiment (Fig. 19). The mask itself can be cut plain, or it can be cut at the edges and given a hairy appearance. It can have large ears or a longer jaw, and the decoration can be as eccentric or extraordinary as you feel like making it. The mask does not have to be painted to look like a real cat. If it is to be worn for a play it can have a realistic sort of treatment, but later examples of mask will be more suitable for stage work. The present example can be like all the exercises so far suggested, and can be just another opportunity for exciting experiment in pattern and colour on an interesting shape.

If you find that you are able to make some attractive cat faces, you might look around the house to see where you can place them as decorations. A cat's face pinned to the door of a serving hatch between the kitchen and the dining room makes an interesting thing for a visitor to wonder about. A row of them peering over a stair rail will make a nice greeting for anyone arriving at the front door. It used to be the normal practice to put up decorations only at certain times of the year, but if you are

Fig. 19—The simple mask can progress through various decorative stages, including edge cutting and curling, trimming with extra pieces, and surface painting.

making something interesting and colourful in your home you will almost certainly enjoy an occasional extra decoration. You will probably also give some pleasure to other people, either in your own family or to some of the visitors who must come to your house.

For the best effect in an out-of-season decoration the things you produce should not be too obtrusive in the way you place them around the home. You should try to position the cat heads, for example, so that they only appear to visitors after they have begun to get settled in the room. A dark corner is a good place in which to pin an odd cat, or a place somewhere low down — like the space under a wall table so that the shape is only seen by chance, perhaps when the visitor bends down to pick up something which has fallen on the floor.

These masks are really intended to be worn, and should be made large enough for the face. They can be made larger or smaller, however, to suit the situation. If they are to be used as a decoration their size will depend entirely on where you intend to place them. A decoration in a school or club would call for larger masks than would be needed on the back of a guest room door, or in the room in which you are going to have a party. It is entirely a matter of planning and organising and, if you are going to put the masks around the house, of knowing how far you can go without upsetting someone who might then put a stop to your going on with more exercises.

Shaping the Ear

In the diagram (Fig. 20) a method is illustrated of developing the cat mask by cutting and shaping the ear. The cut should be made along the top of the mask to the centre of the ear, and should be continued upwards through the ear to the centre (A–B).

In this cut none of the paper is removed, but it is possible to pull the corner (A) downwards at the back of the mask. The action of pulling the corner down will introduce a hollow form into the actual ear, and this hollow should, of course, have its opening at the front. When the ear is formed the point (A) should be fixed in position at the back of the mask. The fixture can be made with an adhesive or with a staple from an office-type stapling machine. The stapling machine is a very good and immediate way of making a fixture in paper modelling, particularly if the machine is small enough to make a neat fixture. In mask-making it is necessary to remember that staples should be inserted from the inside, so that any sharp ends which are not completely flat are not likely to scratch the wearer. In any case it is useful to cover any staple on the inside of the mask with a patch of adhesive tape, so that the wearer can be sure that he is not going to find the fixtures uncomfortable. The act of giving form to the ears on this mask will introduce you to a further simple technique in paper modelling. If you want to investigate the technique more fully you should take any

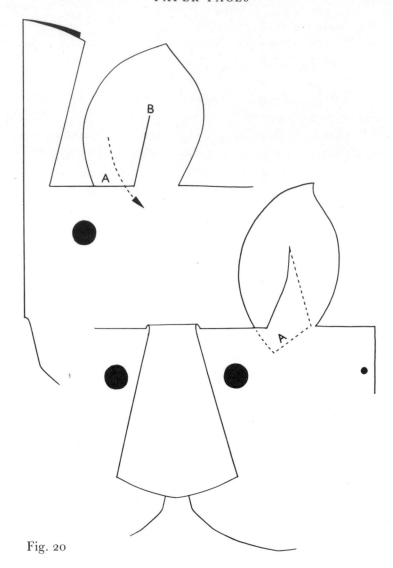

Fig. 20

odd pieces of paper which you have available. If you cut into a flat shape from the edge to the centre and pull the two sides of the cut together, overlapping them, you will raise a form from the original flat shape. The simplest way to demonstrate and understand this technique is to take two circles or discs of paper exactly the same size. In one of the discs you should make a single cut on one radius. If you overlap and fix the two sides of the cut you will raise the disc into a simple cone which will stand up on a flat surface. The uncut shape will remain flat so that although you began with the same shape in both cases you will have two different things in front of you. The uncut disc will naturally remain unaltered, but although nothing is added to, or removed from the second disc, the resultant shape will actually be three-dimensional and free-standing. It will in fact be a very simple piece of sculpture with a form which can be seen from all sides. This technique is one which can be applied in practice when anyone modelling with paper wishes to raise form from a flat shape. The ears can be shaped on any of the masks in order to give slight additional interest to the final effect. It is a simple technique, and the forms made can be used rounded or hollow as the modeller wishes. The technique can be practised and learned by applying it to any of the cat masks in order to make them more interesting than they were in the simple flat shape. Or it can be extended into new mask developments.

The cats can be made larger and more extravagant, like the tigers (Fig. 21). These can be given a bold decorative treatment with suitable stripes and cut edges and with convincingly strong whiskers.

Shaping the Nose

If you have followed the exercises so far your masks will now include form at the front where the nose projects forwards. They will also have concave or hollow forms at the ears, and will have increased visual effect from added pieces of paper cut to

Fig. 21—The basic mask developed into animal shapes can have form at the nose and ears, and can still be a suitable exercise for edge and applied decoration.

represent whiskers or hair. They will also include experiments in edge cutting and painted or drawn decoration.

In spite of these developments they will still be simple masks cut mainly in one piece, but made more exciting visually through your use of techniques which you have learned so far. From this point you can go on to further techniques.

The diagram (Fig. 22) shows a method of cutting the nose in a way which can greatly improve the shape of this feature of the mask. This diagram must again be

Fig. 22

Fig. 23—The one-piece mask can be given enough form and decoration to establish identity and character.

studied closely so that it can be understood before the technique is attempted. The nose is still cut at the top of the head on the folded paper and will, as in previous examples, be bent forwards to the front of the face with the fold reversed. Before bending the nose, you can in this instance cut a shape as in the diagram, and can include a cut from the top (A) into a simple nostril shape. The opening for the nostril should be cut out similar to the shape printed in black on the diagram. When you have bent the nose forward to the front of the mask, you can pull the two sides towards the centre at the bottom of the nose. These can be fixed (B) behind the middle shape of the nostril.

This is a further application of the cutting and overlapping technique, and should raise an interesting form at the end of the nose. The complete mask at the right of the illustration (Fig. 23) demonstrates the type of added form this cut will give to a mask.

The development illustrated in the three masks shows also how useful it is, when introducing this type of modelling into the nose, to cut the actual nose shape as broad as possible without obstructing the wearer's vision.

For a neat visual effect the top of the nose at its thinnest point can be pinched into a triangular shape where it joins the main face. This is a refinement of technique in which you must persuade the paper to do what you want it to by manipulating it with your fingers. When you bend the nose forwards, in some instances it might tend to stick out instead of lying down against the face, and it is this simple pinching action which can keep the nose in place where you want it, at the same time as it gives a neat visual finish to the cutting and folding process.

When all the techniques which have been described so far are included in one mask shape, the single piece of flat paper will have been transformed without much difficulty into a mask of considerable interest like the lion (Fig. 23).

If you have reached this stage you are still making basically the simple mask described in the first exercise. But you are now using a more advanced technique, showing that you have acquired a degree of personal skill.

The masks you have made can be worn by you or your friends. If necessary you can tie them on for each other with short lengths of string, and you can compare your own efforts with those of your friends. If you cannot find anyone to wear the masks with you, you can keep them in your room or, if they are attractive enough, you can mount them as an unusual decoration in some other part of the house.

When you are working in a fairly unusual craft like this you must not expect everyone to be immediately impressed by it, or interested in, everything you do. Some people will like your work, and some people will not be sure. But the important thing is that you will have found some pleasure in doing the exercises you have done already. If this is in any way true you are probably ready to go on to other exercises.

Simple Bird Shapes

The animal shapes already described and illustrated have been evolved as exercises so that anyone interested can be building a vocabulary of simple techniques and skills as they work and make masks.

If you have these skills at your fingertips now, you can change the shape of your work slightly, and can aim to develop them even more fully through a number of mask exercises with new variations. In these you may expect to continue the practice

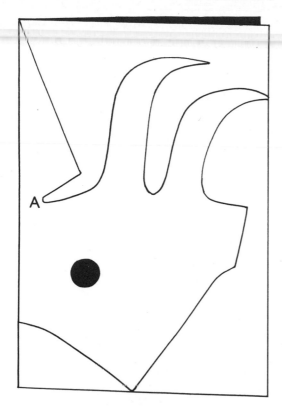

A

Fig. 24

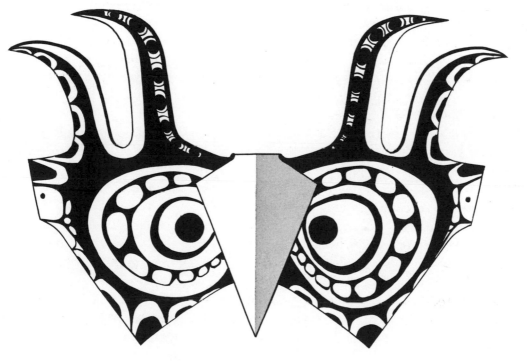

and applications of your skill, at the same time as you begin to develop confidence and your own personal style in treatment and decoration.

If it is possible to cut a nose at the top, and to incorporate it by bending it forward into a mask, it must be possible to do something similar with a range of masks based on bird-like shapes in which the nose becomes a beak.

A simple pointed beak can be cut as in previous exercises at the top of the mask (Fig. 24). The point of this shape must be at the top of the folded paper, and the base of the beak will join on to the main shape. A slight gap or extension piece should be included at the base of the beak (A), so that the beak can be bent easily forward without undue resistance from the width of paper at the base of the beak. If this gap is not included the width of paper at this point is inclined to make a neat fold difficult, and the bird masks can at this early stage look clumsy and unconvincing. This is why the thickness at the bottom of the beak should be reduced to a minimum, at the same time as it must remain strong enough to keep the beak on the mask even when it is worn. To make a bird mask in which the beak tears off quite soon after the mask is completed will be annoying and time-wasting, and it is necessary to find out by experiment with the actual paper or card you are using how much can be safely cut away, and how much must be left to hold the beak and main mask together with adequate strength.

Bird masks are excellent for decorative treatment, both as applied and as cut decoration. When you cut a beak as in Fig. 24 you will have paper at the top sides of the mask which can be incorporated and used as a decorative feature, particularly when it is cut into a crest or feather-like shape. Applied and edge decorations (Fig. 25) should include simple bird-like treatments with bold shapes and details which are not too fussy. These masks can, of course, be particularly suitable for experiments with bright colours, and you can find plenty of suggestions to work from by looking both at birds and at coloured illustrations of species you do not usually find in your own neighbourhood.

After the first exercises in which you will cut your beak shapes as simple inverted triangles, you can experiment with different shaped beaks in order to make various types of bird. If you can find ideas in books, or better still by looking for birds with unusual visual qualities either in their natural surroundings or at a zoo, you will find that this simple mask is very easy to develop.

Exaggerated visual effects, like extravagant plumage or extra large beaks, can be included in the simple shape, and can provide opportunities for much fun and experiment. Masks with larger effects (Fig. 26) are best made in good quality paper which has adequate support in itself. The larger effects can be wasted if the paper is limp to start with and is further weakened by cutting.

The masks illustrated (Fig. 26) are cut in cartridge paper, and rely entirely on their own shapes for support. For really large effects it is of course necessary to start

Fig. 25—Simple bird masks can be cut in a variety of shapes from the single piece of paper and can be made visually effective with surface or applied decorative treatment.

with a large piece of paper, and in the process of working at the mask you must expect to cut away large areas of the original shape. Care should be taken not to remove too much of the shape from one part of the mask, and in your early planning you should aim to include as much of the original as you can, without making the shape dull. You can make simple designs and preliminary drawings, or even full-size patterns in wrapping paper or newspaper before embarking on the actual masks. It is also possible to draw the mask on folded paper, altering your drawing until you are finally satisfied, and after cutting to reverse the whole thing so that the cleaner side comes to the front.

As your work becomes more advanced you will find it useful to plan and design, and to experiment before using your scissors on the paper. When you design it is of course only necessary to work on one half of the paper, because you know that after cutting it double on the fold the mask will be symmetrical when you open it out.

When you are using large paper for simple masks which have large features, you should carefully save any paper which you cut away and which may be potentially useful as trimmings for later experiment.

In one of the masks (Fig. 26) cuts are made into the actual surface of the mask, and the cut pieces are curled forwards from the flat shape. This surface decoration

Fig. 26—Variations on the one-piece bird shapes can be achieved by a bold approach to the original cutting, and with experimental decorative treatment.

can be visually effective but is difficult to manage with an ordinary pair of scissors. The cuts must be made with a sharp knife, and care must be taken to see that the knife does not slip, and that the thin cut pieces are not torn from the mask when you curl them.

By this stage, if you have really made a determined attempt to experiment with shapes, you should find it possible to make a range of very attractive bird masks. From this point you can begin to consider the business of planning and cutting masks into really specific shapes.

If you are developing a personal ability in mask-making you will almost certainly be asked on some future occasion to make masks for someone else. Some of these requests will be for masks for plays or other special occasions, and you will be asked to form the masks into recognisable shapes. It is clearly not possible in this type of work to make shapes which stand the remotest chance of being mistaken for the real thing, but a mask required for a play will have to establish the character in a simple and direct way, and must be planned so that the final result will convey the right effect in the best way possible.

After the work you have attempted so far, you should begin to realise that although there are no rules in mask-making, you will find that whatever you set out to do will work if you do it the right way. This is a simple principle which can be applied to most kinds of practical work.

In subsequent exercises you will see that in most cases the intention has been to solve the problems involved in making a particular kind of mask. As you work the exercises you should try to understand exactly what is required in each case, and the processes which are applied to make the ultimate shape of the mask meet the requirements. If you can follow the processes both in the idea and in the practical stages, you will appreciate the stages described and will find it easier to make your own solutions when you have to tackle mask-making problems of your own.

Chicken and Crow

This is an exercise in which you can compare the visual effects of different treatments. Both the shapes are cut on a centre fold, and both of them are designed as masks incorporating eyes and a beak. But the final effect in each case should be contrasted enough to make the chicken acceptably different from the crow.

In making any particular shape of mask the first stage of the problem is to consider the simple character of the shape you want, trying to pick out exactly what distinguishes it from any other species. If you can look at the shape and pick out the right characteristics you will have begun to solve the problem. If you can then translate what you have discovered about the shape into a series of workable processes which can be applied to a simple mask you will be able to carry your solution through to the end product.

The chicken is a fairly harmless creature, but compared with other birds it has a cruel, though not very large, beak. If you take the folded shape (Fig. 27) and draw the beak (A), you will find that you have a large area of paper left at the top of the mask. This area (B) can be conveniently used as the basis for an exaggerated comb-like shape, and can be cut into a series of points at the top. When you cut it you should make it appear to point forward, otherwise it might take on the unwanted appearance of a plume.

The chicken will require a feathered appearance where possible, and part of the original mask can be cut to give this effect at the edges (C). Chickens tend to have fleshy bag-like shapes under the eyes, and the bottom front part of the mask can be cut to convey this effect in the simplest way, (D).

After you have cut the shape and folded the beak downwards as in previous exercises, the mask can be further developed by the addition of simple curved forms

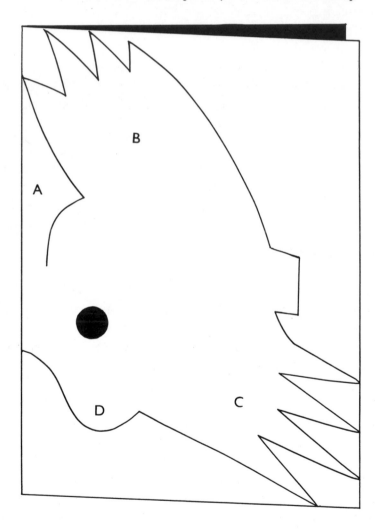

Fig. 27

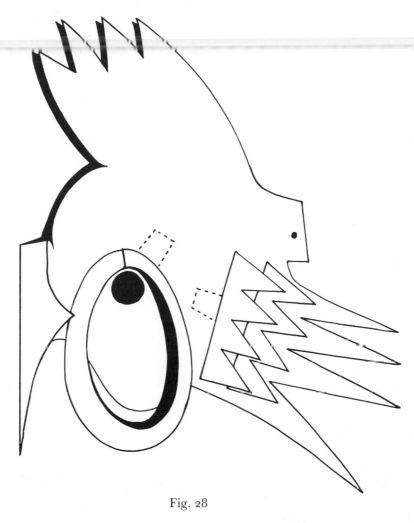

Fig. 28

to the eyes to stress the drooping effect. These can be paper additions cut into circle-like shapes and secured at the top of the eyes with tabs through slots into the back of the mask (Fig. 28). Further simple feathery shapes can be used to build up more form in the mask. The flattest mask can be transformed into a shape with real form by the addition of three or four strips of paper with cut points. These can be made from offcuts left over from previous exercises, and should be fixed over each other, starting at the back, so that the one nearest the front is the last. This method of fixing will mean that each one will hide the fixture point of the one it covers, and the mask will be kept as neat as possible. After the shapes have been fixed the points can be slightly curled so that they will make shadows and will add to the visual effect. The processes are illustrated (Fig. 29), and the final version of the mask, although it is in fact very far removed from the real thing, should be a simplified version of a droopy-eyed bird which might, if we are not too critical, be acceptable as a chicken.

To understand the processes involved in planning and making this mask it is necessary to appreciate in the first place that, as in other crafts, there is a certain limited potential in the simple paper mask, and that because of this limit it is necessary to find a simple and fairly immediate statement in visual terms. In the case of the chicken the characteristics attempted include the sharp beak, the comb and the droopy eyes.

You will be able to see how well this has solved the problem by contrasting it with a different bird. A bird shape which conveys the appearance of a blackbird or crow requires a larger beak, and in this instance it is rather more important to include both lower and upper beaks.

The diagram (Fig. 30) can be read from the bottom upwards. The face part of the mask is cut on the fold, with the holes for eyes in the usual place. In this exercise

Fig. 29—It should be possible to establish a particular identity in a mask by selecting the main characteristics of a shape.

the paper must be rather longer than you have previously used because the beak, which has a long, pointed form, has an extra large extension piece from the top of the actual mask. The beak is again positioned in the diagram on the fold at the top of the mask, and if you turn the diagram sideways you will see that it is drawn with the lower beak shape included.

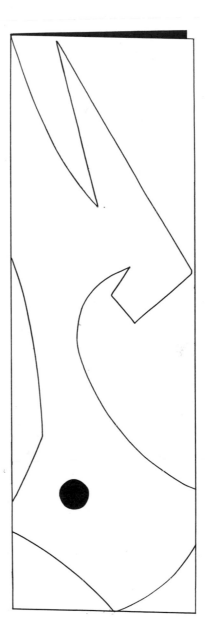

Fig. 30

The cut-out shape (Fig. 31) should be gummed along the lower edge of the bottom beak—shaded part of the diagram—and stuck together on the inside. This sticking

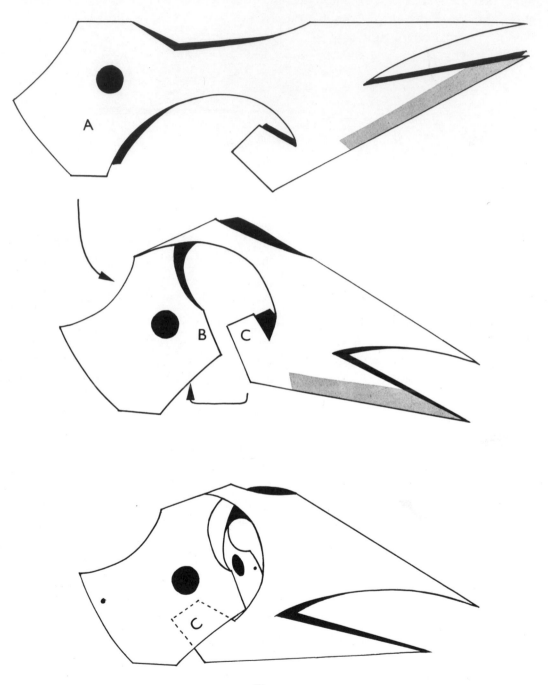

Fig. 31

process will give you the two sides of the lower beak joined as they should be at the bottom.

When the beak has been fixed, the mask can be bent into shape. To do this you must take the actual mask shape (A) and push it downwards to the beak. The direction of this movement is indicated by the top arrow. As you bring this shape down and into position you must reverse the fold so that it is pointing forwards (B).

The flaps at the ends of the lower beak can be pulled out to the sides and fixed at the back of the mask (C).

This mask is an example of a simple paper manipulation in which a flat shape is treated in such a way that it can be locked into a raised form which is adequately strong. At a first reading the cutting and raising process will almost certainly appear complicated and difficult. But in any subject drawings and instructions which are to be used as a basis for practical work must be examined carefully and must be fully understood before any work is started.

The crow's head is not difficult. It is a shape which is folded downwards from the middle. You will find that it helps when you want to fold an already established fold to cut away some part of the original paper. You can see that this has been done in this exercise at the top of the diagram (Fig. 31).

Fig. 32—The flat paper can be made to project forward by folding and fixing
a basic shape.

When you have understood this process you will see that the crow's head is cut and made up as a simple shape with a large pointed beak. In the chicken's mask the beak had no lower part. But in this instance, since as with many other birds the head is almost all beak, it is necessary to find a way of making the beak as effectively as possible. You will see in later exercises that in a bird mask a lower beak can in fact be added separately, but in this particular exercise the problem of the beak is solved in one cut.

Since the beak is cut proportionately larger than the face of the mask it will make an immediate impact when it is worn, and it is only necessary to cut the mask out of black paper for the end product to read as an acceptable version of the blackbird, and for it to be quite different from the chicken. The black shape can be decorated, when it is made up, with cut paper in contrasting colour (Fig. 32), or it can be used as an interesting experiment for colour work.

If you paint a pattern on a black ground you will find it necessary to take rather special care about your colour. It depends what sort of paints you use, but in most cases either you will have to make your colours very strong or you will have to mix them in a certain way, possibly with white, in order to make it possible for them to be seen against the black. This is good experience for you, and if you experiment enough you will find that some interesting pattern contrasts are possible on the black background. For later experiment the shape with the two parts of the beak cut in one can be adapted as a basis for more bird masks. In comparison with any previous method used it is clearly more difficult to master, but the end result is different and the final effect can be rather more mature and convincing than the simple pointed beak which you used in previous exercises.

In this exercise the flat paper was raised to a fairly extensive form at the front of the mask. If it is possible to do this with one shape, it is possible to apply the same technique in order to find other shapes. The only thing you really have to do is to accept the fact that most things are possible if you go about them in the right way. You can examine this more fully in the next two exercises.

Pig

To make the pig mask (Fig. 33) you must use the techniques introduced in previous exercises. In this case the nose is cut with a characteristic shape, a round end on a short but thick muzzle. When this is bent forward the character can be further established by modelling the end of the nose so that the round part is flat, although the nose itself

Fig. 33

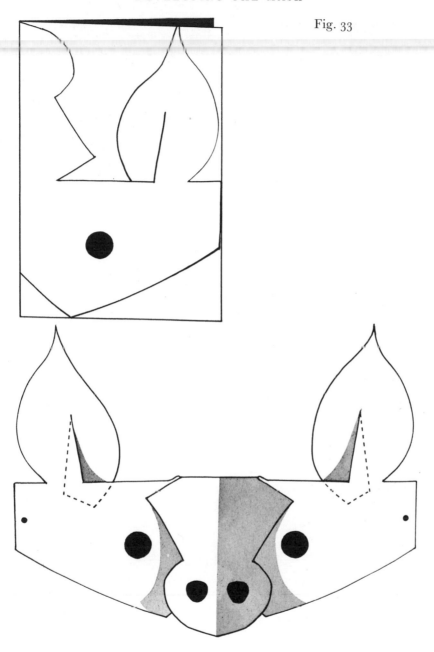

is projecting forward. This will mean folding the end of the nose and pinching it tightly together so that it will stay in position.

Large ears can be cut and modelled as in previous exercises, and the visual effect can be developed to suit yourself. You can make, if you like, very much larger ears

Fig. 34—Most head shapes are possible from a single piece of paper. In this instance the nose
and ears treated in the right way should establish the identity of the mask.

which will flop forward over the face after cutting. This mask is not quite so immediate
in impact as some which you might have attempted previously, and any applied
decoration would require careful thought, so that the shape is not completely lost
under the pattern and colour.

It will help if you look at the mask before decorating it, in order to establish
points where decoration will assist in establishing character as well as adding to the
attraction of the mask. This is a stage you should now begin to think about in your
work; how, for example, certain forms might be assisted by the use of colour and tone,
and how parts of the mask ought to be stressed in preference to others.

The hollow shapes of the ears, for example, can be made to look actually deeper
than they really are if you paint them with a darker tone of colour than the rest of
the face. The eyes can similarly be made to look as though they are set in sockets.

You can compare in the illustration (Fig. 34) the differences between the undeco-
rated mask, the mask with painted decoration and the mask with painted and cut
decoration. In the plain mask the eyes are merely holes in the paper. We know these
are necessary for the wearer, but when we add a little painted decoration they become

slightly more real. You can try various effects on the eyes, darker or lighter colours and different outline shapes.

The mask illustrated with cut decoration has a surface treatment similar to that suggested in the earlier chicken mask. In this case you can again make the form and surface more interesting by cutting patterns of hair-like shapes and bending or curling them forward. These cuts, which must be made with a fairly sharp knife, provide visual interest because the gap left when they are curled forward leaves a contrasting dark opening at the back. When this contrast is repeated, as it is when the cuts are made in a pattern, it provides a visually interesting textured effect.

The use of a sharp knife in paper modelling need not be a handicap to anyone attempting the exercises. If a knife which is sharp is incorrectly used it will obviously be dangerous. But anyone who wants to use a tool in a craft should be interested enough to learn to use it properly.

With a sharp knife it is necessary in the first place to have a suitable surface on which to cut. A thick card or hardboard off-cut will be good enough, and the paper to be cut should be placed on it and held firmly with one hand. The positioning of the free hand is important, since this is the one which will be cut if the knife slips. A strict rule which can be applied in every case is that the free hand must never be in the path of the cutting edge of the knife. It must always be behind the sharp edge, and when the cut is being made the knife must be drawn away from the hand which holds the paper. If this turns out to be awkward or difficult in some cases, the paper should be turned until the action can be carried out comfortably and without danger.

If this safety precaution becomes an accepted part of the modeller's technique, and if the rule is observed scrupulously so that it becomes automatic, a sharp knife will be no more dangerous than a pair of scissors. When the free hand is behind the blade, an incorrect cut or a slipping knife can only damage the paper or the cutting surface. When a sharp knife becomes an acceptable part of your personal equipment, and when the right sort of technique has become automatic, you will have reached a stage of real ability in the craft of modelling with paper, and should be able to go on without any limit. There is still, however, plenty of scope for anyone who feels unable to use a sharp knife and prefers to carry on with a pair of scissors.

Rat

In almost any piece of paper there is somewhere an interesting shape. Although it may appear dull and lifeless when it is flat, it can — given the right treatment — be made to do interesting and unexpected things. This is because it is a material which

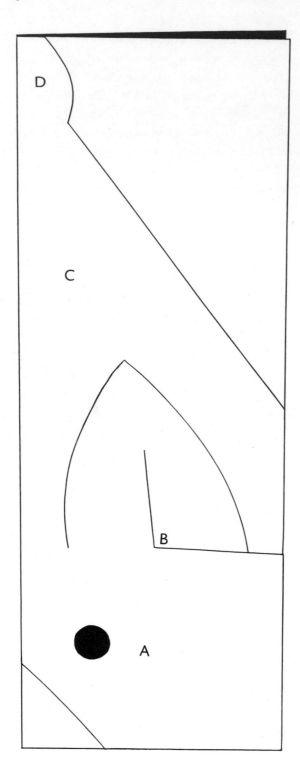

Fig. 35

is relatively easy to manipulate. It can be turned and twisted, and curled or folded, and of course it can be cut and rearranged.

Many different masks can be made up from flat paper by cutting and folding in a particular way. When you have had a certain amount of practice you will find, in fact, that there is a great deal of potential form in a flat piece of paper. This is demonstrated as a final exercise in this section by the Rat (Fig. 35) which illustrates a way of using almost all the paper in order to find an interesting form.

The diagrams must again be looked at closely and understood as you cut and raise the form. The original fold of paper need not have an exact or measured size, but as a guide it should be roughly half as large again as this page. After folding the paper through the middle on its longer length you should place it in front of you with the folded edge on your left.

The mask shape used in all the exercises so far should be drawn at the bottom of the paper (Fig. 35 A), and you can include fairly large ears. These should again be cut along the top of the mask to the centre, and in this instance the cut should be made from the outer edge of the mask. The cut should then turn upwards through the middle of the ear (B), so that the right-angle of the cut will allow you to raise a hollow form in the ear through the technique of overlapping.

The nose is again included at the top of the folded shape, but this time it is in the form of a very long muzzle (C) with a rounded snout at its end (D). When the mask is made up, this long snout will project well forward from the mask and will give the long thin effect which is needed for a rat.

To draw this on your fold of paper before you do any cutting you should notice that the simple mask (A) can be drawn the same size as in previous exercises. The right-hand side of the muzzle on the unfolded edge of the paper is approximately halfway up the side, and the tip of the ear in the middle of the muzzle is slightly above this point.

After drawing and cutting the shape you must look closely at the diagram (Fig. 36) in order to see how the form should be raised. The muzzle must be folded forwards at the front of the mask (arrow A) with the fold reversed, and the bottom of the muzzle must be opened out and secured to the main mask at both sides (B). This fixture can be made with tabs inserted through slots, or it can be a stuck or stapled fixture disguised with added cut paper (C).

You will notice when you manage this process successfully that although you bend a large part of the shape forwards the ears will remain in position at the top of the mask. Because of the way they are cut in the original shape the ears leave gaps in the sides of the muzzle when the form is folded so that it is possible for the wearer to see through the eye holes. This is a deliberate and necessary technique, in which the need to cut a particular shape has been exploited to advantage so that a problem has been solved. If these parts of the muzzle were not removed it might be difficult

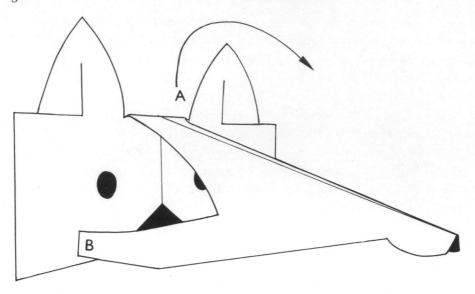

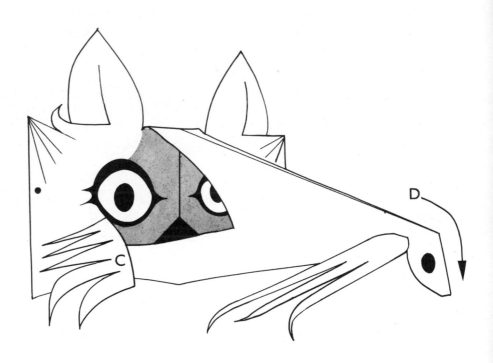

Fig. 36

for the wearer to see, and the act of raising the form would have presented a new problem which would have required solving before the mask was wearable. The rounded snout at the end of the muzzle can be bent downwards (arrow D) and stapled into position. The fixture at this point can be hidden with whiskers cut from the paper left over in the original shape.

To add to the general effect you can fold and fix the ears to give form, and you can paint those parts of the mask which you think will add to its impact. A final rat-like touch can be given by adding two large teeth at the tip of the nose (Fig. 37), which is in the case of a rat a characteristic and helpful feature.

In this exercise you have seen how a flat piece of paper may be raised to an interesting form when it is cut and manipulated in the right way. It should never be necessary when you are trying this to buckle or crumple the paper, nor should you try to bully it into shape. If the paper is not responding to your efforts you are almost certainly not putting your cuts or folds in the right places, and before ruining the paper you should stop and consider exactly what it is you want it to do.

Fig. 37—Considerable form can be raised in one piece of paper if it is cut and folded in a suitable way. The rat is cut on a central fold and can be made in one piece, with additions for whiskers and teeth.

The creative process can be attempted in a hurry, or it can be as slow and deliberate as you like. As an aspiring craftsman you should aim at all times to be in control of the materials, never letting them at any time take over and do something you do not intend — unless, by some chance, what happens by accident looks like being something you can turn to your own advantage. If this is the case then you should be ready to pause and consider how you might exploit any new discovery.

When you have made a number of the masks already suggested, you will be familiar with the principle of using the simple flat mask which has parts projecting forward to make the shape. At some point during the process of working at the exercises you might have begun to experiment with shapes of your own. It does not matter if these are sometimes not quite as good as you would like them to be. They will be your own shapes, unique and personal to you, and as such they will be valuable stages in your development as a craftsman.

If you now have the urge to make something which has not been included so far in the exercises, you must use the techniques you have learned and must experiment until you get the shape right.

If you want to invent creatures of your own, you are free to do so. You can, if you like, make a whole range of imaginary birds or beasts in the most fantastic shapes and colours. The techniques which have been demonstrated so far can be applied in exactly the same way as you have already applied them. Everything will not of course be straightforward and simple from that point. In any sort of creative work the most capable and experienced craftsmen meet, and have to overcome, new problems as they work. You will meet difficulties, and must expect to have vexing moments when the paper does not go quite right, and your mask does not look as you intended it to. But in any creative and experimental work there have to be moments of failure as well as success, and it is necessary to accept and examine the failures in order to go on to the next process.

If you have become interested in the work so far you will want to go on experimenting with human and animal masks. You will make them for your own personal pleasure, or for parties or plays and special occasions. As you work you will find yourself looking at things in a new way. People will be more than just strangers, and you will see someone new and interesting every day because you will be looking for things to use — a new shape for a face, or an interesting detail which you can enlarge or exaggerate.

If you have enjoyed decorating the masks, and want to go on experimenting with colours and shapes, you can go on looking for patterns and interesting visual effects in the world around you. You will find them everywhere. You will find them in everything in nature from shells and objects from the seashore, to leaves and plants. Every flower goes through exciting visual changes as it develops from its first bud to its final form when the seeds are dispersed. There are patterns in rocks and patterns in the sky. A simple moth or beetle, usually treated as a nuisance in the house, might have the most exciting and extravagant patterns and colouring on its small shape if you look at it closely enough. Wherever we happen to be there is usually some sort of pattern which has been established by nature. In modern times it can be an interesting venture in itself merely to find these, and any of them which we find might serve as a basis for the development of our own work in colour.

There are many other sources of pattern which are worth investigating. Men make patterns, sometimes deliberately and sometimes by accident. A piece of machinery has a purpose; wheels and rods or other parts which move in a given way to perform a specific function. But if we forget what the machine does or what it is intended to make, and if we look at the shapes—and the shapes behind the shapes—we might find interesting visual contrasts, with lines and squares and circles, doing in hard materials something which we could do in our own way with pencil or paint. We have to remember that we are looking only for ideas for combining different shapes in interesting ways to make exciting and new sorts of pattern, and remembering this we can, of course, alter or rearrange the shapes we see to suit ourselves.

There are other man-made patterns all around us besides those made by the component parts of machinery. The skyline with chimneys and aerials—we can see this sometimes from the room in which we are working—can be an interesting arrangement of shapes. If you walk across a railway bridge and look down you can sometimes see ready-made patterns in the rails and junctions. There are patterns everywhere, and looking for them can be enormously rewarding. If you are aware of patterns in the world around, you will never have a dull moment, even when you have to go to places and do things you really do not want to.

After a number of exercises on the simple mask shape you can begin to look for a technique which will extend the range of your work. If you have become fairly able to make the sort of masks which have to be tied on, you should be ready to go on to a type of work which has more scope and more durability.

For plays and other special occasions like fêtes and organised gatherings it might be useful to make masks which can be worn as heads, and which will be strong enough to be worn on a number of occasions, for example at rehearsals or repeat performances.

To do this we must extend the original simple mask into a basic shape which can be exploited and developed more fully. The basic shape should still be possible in thick paper or in card, and its development should also be possible in the same materials. The following exercises illustrate the development and use of a basic shape. The examples illustrated are intended for you to have fun at the same time as you learn to work with, and manage, the basic shape.

BASIC SHAPE

A suitable basic shape for a more advanced type of mask-making is illustrated in the diagram (Fig. 40). This is best made in thin card, but if card is not available it will work just as well in good quality paper.

If you look closely at the diagram you will see that it is cut on a central fold, and that it does actually include the familiar mask shape at the bottom. This should be the same size as in previous exercises, and comparison between this and other diagrams will give you some idea of the size of the flaps which are included at the top and sides.

The extension at the top must be long enough to go over the top of the head of the wearer, and those at the sides must be long enough to go round the head and overlap at the back. When the side flaps are overlapped they can at the same time be adjusted to a size to fit the wearer and can be fixed together (Fig. 39B). The top flap can also be adjusted over the head and can be folded over the side flaps and fixed (A). When the flaps are fixed in the right position for the wearer it will be possible for the mask to be worn like a hat (Fig. 38).

Fig. 38—The basic mask can be developed into a shape on which to build more elaborate masks and heads. It should be adjusted to fit the wearer.

Fig. 39

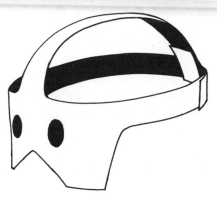

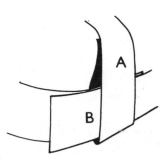

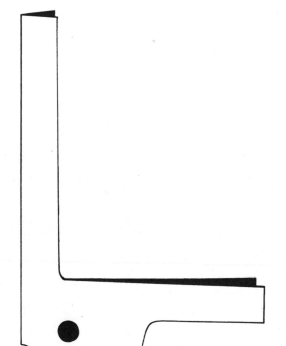

Fig. 40

The adjustment of the flaps on the mask is very important, and some care should be taken to see that it can be done satisfactorily in the early stages. The mask itself must fit comfortably on the bridge of the nose, and the wearer must be able to see clearly through the holes cut for the eyes without having to lift his hand to adjust the mask every few minutes. If the adjustment is right, it will be possible for the wearer to move freely about when the basic shape is made up into even the most elaborate mask, without any risk of his losing the mask, and it will be useful in play productions where unhampered movements are necessary to the action.

When the basic shape is made up satisfactorily it can be developed into a variety of interesting heads. Almost any mask can be developed on the shape, and a really skilled ability in mask-making can be gained through practising with the basic shape and with some of the various technical processes involved. These can be practised and learned through some of the following exercises, in which animal shapes are examined and simplified into workable masks.

The processes involved are described and illustrated, and you must in each case study the diagrams and try to understand the techniques which are used to make the basic shape into a mask.

The photographs in most instances show the mask in various stages of development, from the plain form which is illustrated in the diagrams to the decorated end product. They are made in combinations of paper and card, and are in each case developed on the basic shape illustrated (Fig. 40).

The technique of scoring, which will be used on a number of occasions in the exercises in this section of the book, will be familiar to some people. But anyone who has not already had an opportunity to use the technique should stop at this stage and make a point of learning it. It can be mastered in a few minutes, and can be practised on any odd scraps of paper.

Any piece of paper can be folded, but in order to make the fold as nearly perfect as possible, and exactly where it is required, the paper modeller will take a knife or scissor blade and will cut very slightly into the surface of the paper along the length of the line to be folded. This cut must not at any point go right through the paper, and the technique must be practised until you can get the feel of the exact pressure required. This will depend on the thickness of the paper and on the sharpness of the blade, and is entirely a matter of practice and experience.

The first practice scores can be made straight, using a ruler as a guide. They should be made on the outer side of the paper, so that when the paper is folded the two sides of the fold are bent away from the score, allowing the surface to open slightly at the cut.

A curved score can be made just as effectively as a straight one, but it must be made freehand. It can be made using a pencil line as a guide, but after a little practice it should be possible to make curved scores with a careful and free movement of the hand holding the blade. The advantage of scoring can be demonstrated by making a simple curved score and bending the paper on it in order to raise form. If you try to raise the same form on another piece of paper without the preliminary score you will find it is impossible to do it with any degree of neatness.

Tiger — Lion

To make a mask on the basic shape it is necessary to project the features forward. This projection requires a support, which can be made in the form of a simple muzzle shape (Fig. 41). This should be cut double on the fold, as illustrated in the diagram. The folded shape will give immediate strength and support when the muzzle is fixed

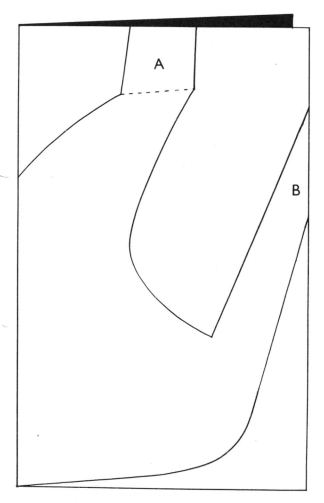

Fig. 41

at the front of the mask (Fig. 44). The muzzle should be fixed at the front of the head with the flaps (Fig. 41 A), which should be scored and folded at the dotted lines. After folding and scoring the muzzle should be opened slightly, so that the flaps can be fixed at the front on each side of the upper band of the basic shape (Fig. 44 A).

If you are working from the diagrams you will have at this stage a head with the forward projecting muzzle fixed at the top. The sides of the muzzle should also be fixed at (B) on each cheek. When the fixtures are being made care should be taken to see that the centre line of the muzzle is as nearly as possible over the centre of the

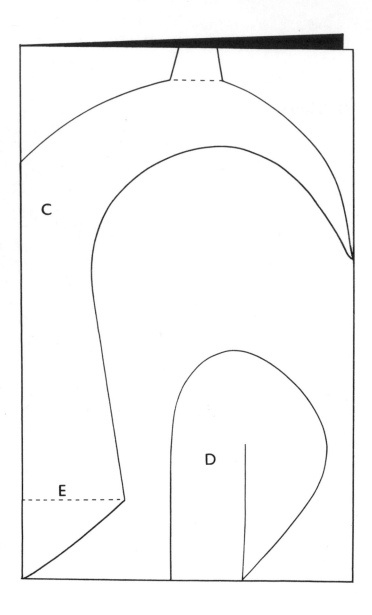

Fig. 42

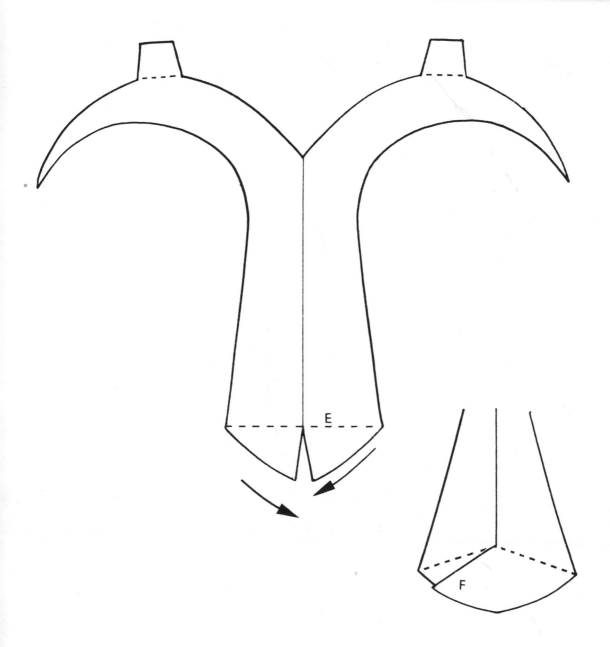

Fig. 43

basic shape, and that it is fixed without an odd, lop-sided look. This is merely a matter of looking at the shape as you make the fixtures, and holding it in the correct position. The four fixing points will keep the muzzle firmly in place on the mask and, if the cuts are right, the two pieces together should be quite strong and rigid.

When it is in position the muzzle can be used as a support for a nose. A suitable shape is illustrated (Fig. 42 C) with fixing flaps at the top. These should again be scored at the dotted line in order to make a fixture point on the mask.

The nose shape is illustrated with exaggerated curved eyebrows, which will assist the visual effect of the finished mask.

The score (E) should be made across the bottom of the nose, and a cut should be made from the bottom of the shape, through the centre line to this score. This cut will enable you to overlap the sides of the lower nose (arrows Fig. 43) into a raised form. This form must be fixed by gumming or with a staple (Fig. 43 F).

The process of cutting and overlapping the nose will give it a blunt-ended and visually interesting shape, which will be strengthened and supported by its central fold.

The nose can be made up and placed on the mask on top of the muzzle. When it is in a suitable position it can be fixed at the top on each side, using the flaps incorporated into the eyebrows in the original cut.

Since there could be an unnecessary waste of paper in cutting the nose and eyebrows on the fold, ear shapes can be cut from the same section (Fig. 42 D). These can be simple, curved shapes which can have a cut to the centre, so that they can be shaped before being fixed to the mask. After they have had form raised as in previous exercises, they can be fixed at the top of the basic shape on each side, to the rear of the nose and muzzle fixtures.

To the beginner this process of cutting and assembling the mask might appear complicated, and the organisation involved might be intimidating. It is not necessary to be timid or hesitant in attempting the exercise because the process is quite simple and straightforward. It is a solution to a design problem which was the starting point for the exercise. A flat head shape has to be extended forward into a mask. Added shapes have to be cut and placed in position, both to provide support and to make the total effect visual. The support for the nose is provided by the muzzle, which is in itself cut at the front to suggest the jowl-like shapes of an animal's jaw. It is also partly cut away in its main form so that anyone wearing the mask can still see through the eye holes.

The nose form is cut flat, but the process of overlapping it at the lower end will make the fold stand up sharply, so that the nose will have two clearly defined sides, and will be suitably shaped at the nostrils.

The large eyebrows will make interesting curves over the eyes. These forms can be moulded into place and can be stuck in position with a little gum. Their positioning

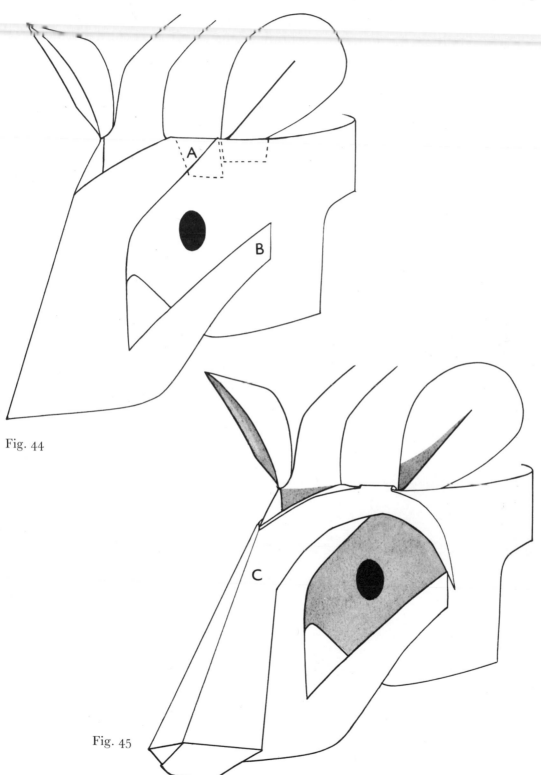

Fig. 44

Fig. 45

should create interesting shadows under the eyebrows and should give emphasis to the eyes, which can be painted as though they are in sockets. The shadows under the eyebrows, and those between the separate shapes, will introduce added suggestions of form into the mask.

The head made in this exercise is illustrated in three versions (Fig. 46). The plain version in the centre is the one described, and this can be further developed into a specific form. The tiger on the left has a few added whiskers and hairy shapes, and is painted in simple bands of colour. The colour factor in this instance can be the yellow, black, white arrangement which is correct for the subject, and this can in itself be an interesting and valuable colour experience. The shape can be easily developed into a lion with a more elaborate treatment of the hair and mane. The large cut shape of the mane in the illustration is an example of immediate and simple effect. It is cut

Fig. 46—Heads made on the basic shape can be developed with simple added shapes. The decorative treatment of this type of head can be simple and direct but visually exciting.

double and fixed at the top, and the point of fixture is hidden by a few exaggerated curls. If the lion is to be worn in a play it will be necessary to cut more shapes for the mane and to position these so that they hang down over the back of the head. If they are arranged carefully it should be possible in most cases to hide the point of fixture.

This type of head is suitable for plays and dramatic work because although it masks most of the face of the wearer it actually rests on the nose, and the wearer can speak with the mask on. In any of the exercises developed on this basic shape there is no part immediately obstructing the nose or mouth, and any of the heads can be worn, even when it is necessary for the wearer to speak lines.

If the right adjustment is made to the bands of the basic shape it should be possible for the head to be slipped on and off almost as easily as a hat. At the same time, when it is on it should remain properly in position even when the wearer has to make quite violent movements.

If movement of the head causes the mask to slip about, so that the wearer has to keep straightening it, it will be necessary to make slight adjustments at the back of the basic shape. This should be done during the preparation and making processes, and it is quite usual to have a number of fittings before the finished head can be finally accepted. The adjustments might have to be made at various stages in the process because the addition of extra parts as decorative features is quite likely to alter the actual size of the mask, and final adjustments should only be made when the mask is complete and ready for wearing.

If this type of mask is made for use in a play it can be stored between the times when it is in use by having strings attached to the headband, so that the mask can be hung from a peg or from a line stretched across the room.

The masks illustrated have been made in paper and thin card, but these and others in later exercises can, if required, be made stronger and more durable. For a lasting head, and one which is visually of unusual interest, the component shapes can be cut in card and can be covered with a layer of material or sacking as the mask is put together. The materials can be stuck to the card with paste or with size, and can be moulded to the shape as the form is raised.

Interesting hairy effects can be made by fraying the edges of the sacking, or by cutting and adding extra shapes—like the lion's mane—from the same material.

String, wool or rope can be combined with the original materials to make a visual effect. They can contrast in colour and texture and can be fixed to the head with simple stitches. Offcuts of patterned and coloured dress or furnishing materials can be used as a covering in place of sacking. These can be selected and arranged to give exciting visual effects. Scraps of material are usually available in a large range of tones and colours and the simple sculptured shapes of the masks you will make in this section can be decorated with various combinations of pattern and colour.

Various pastes and adhesives can be used for sticking material to the card as you make the masks, and anyone interested has only to experiment in order to find the best and most easily obtained adhesive. Some pastes will work well, but in some cases the card might buckle and distort the shape, and a different sort of glue will have to be found. As a general rule a simple paste similar to that used by decorators is likely to work well enough, and will usually not leave unpleasant stains on the finished mask.

If you stick pieces of material to any of the masks you make you will be able to compare the visual effect of painted card with the different finish which is possible with stuck fabrics. Some offcuts of fabric will be exciting because of their colour and pattern, but you should look also for others which have interesting woven effects. If you can find some materials which are very rough to handle, and can decorate some of your masks with these, you will see new and exciting visual effects as the textured material picks up the light on different planes or surfaces of the mask. A richly textured material will also in some instances introduce the right sort of skin-like effect, and can be used in fact to deliberately soften the rather sharp and angular quality of contrasting paper surfaces.

For the right sort of visual effect at the eyes it is essential that the eyeballs should be painted white, with darker pupils. This is the way most eyes are coloured, and it is desirable that the eyes and their positioning make an immediate impact on anyone looking at the masks. If the eyes are not clearly painted the head is likely to look blind when it is seen from a distance, and this will tend to make it look unfinished and inadequate. Where the masks are to be used under some form of stage lighting, a dramatic effect can be obtained by sticking sequins at the corners of the eyes. These will appear to flash momentarily as the head is moved, and will introduce a touch of unexpected liveliness into the mask. If sequins are not available small pieces of silver or coloured foil can be used to give the same effect, which might be particularly useful in a play where anyone has to wear the head of a lion or some other impressive creature.

Decorations and other interesting factors which are not included in the examples can be considered and applied anywhere in the work. Large teeth might be thought a useful addition to the creation of a particular effect, and these can be cut from card and added to the finished work. If you feel that it will help with the effect you want, you can cut a large red tongue, and position it so that it appears to be hanging from the mouth. When cutting this it will be necessary to consider making it with flaps so that the shape can be included with concealed fixtures.

When you look at your finished masks, whether you have followed the diagrams exactly, or whether you have branched out with additions of your own, you should be able to see where you have not done enough. If there are gaps or unpleasant shapes you will have to give more thought and time to the work, and will have to experiment with colours and shapes in order to make the mask as effective as you can. If you are not satisfied with the end product you should go on with further experiment, since you should know by now that paper and card can be as effective in their own way as almost any other material.

Cat

The lion mask is a basic animal shape which can be made to change through slight variations into different animals.

The techniques in modelling are often the same when the subject changes, but they have many slight variations for potential different uses, and it is good practice to discover and practise a few simple ways of varying techniques.

In the lion's mask the nose was cut fairly long so that the forward projection of the face should be marked enough to be visually effective. If it is drawn and cut shorter (Fig. 47) it will be slightly less forceful and dramatic, and the shape will be more like a cat than a lion. The shape can be softened further, and a new variation on a technique

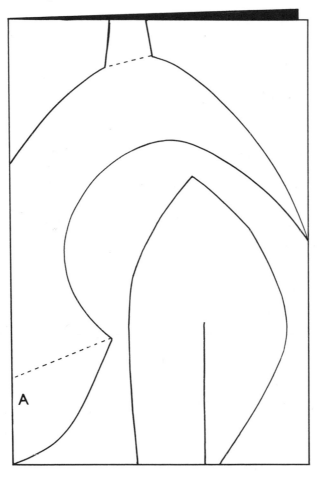

Fig. 47

can be examined, if you round the end of the nose and make the score slope down slightly on both sides towards the centre (Fig. 47 A).

In this case the nose should again be cut from the bottom on the centre line to the score, so that it can be overlapped in order to raise form at the end. If the score has been made as suggested in the diagram, the fold will make the curved part of the nose slope backwards under the main shape. The lower part, where you can paint the nostrils, should be slightly curved by the overlapping process, and the total effect should be to make the mask considerably blunter than in the previous exercise.

The muzzle which will support the nose should be adjusted and cut to a suitable size so that it will fit the shorter nose. It can be the same basic shape as illustrated (Fig. 41), but will have to be shorter in length so that it does not project beyond the end of the nose, and ruin the visual effect. This sort of adjustment will be necessary all the time as you work, and you must be prepared to cut and change as you go along.

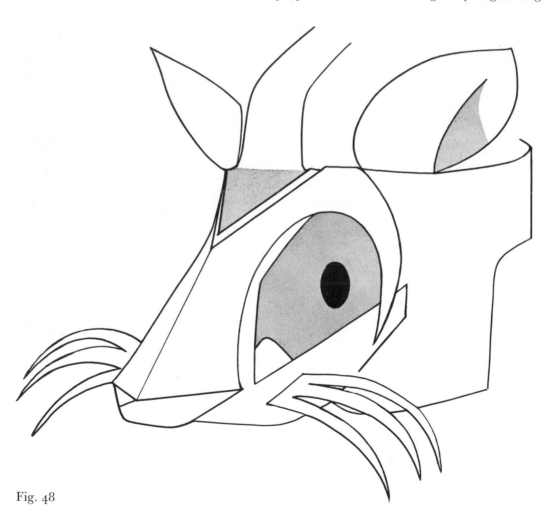

Fig. 48

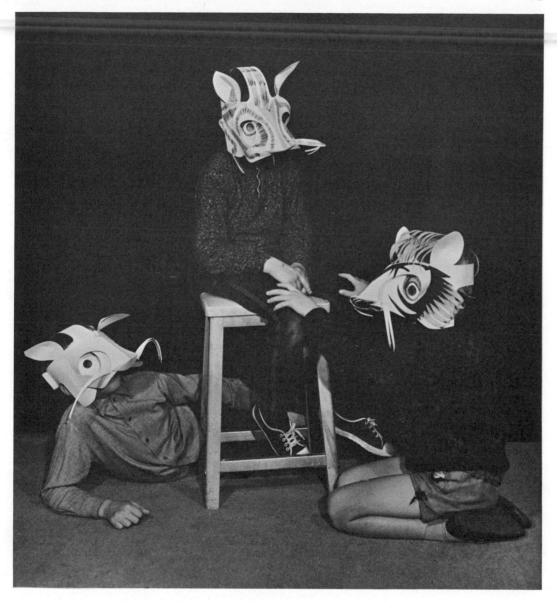

Fig. 49—Cats and other animals are possible on the basic shape, which can be developed
with painted pattern or with added pieces cut in contrasting tones.

The plain mask (Fig. 48) can be put together in the same way as the lion, the ears
having been cut out of the original fold for the nose.

It can be decorated (Fig. 49) with a painted effect, or it can have added paper
decoration. The cat illustrated has cut paper additions in simple contrasting tones,

6

and these are placed so that the visual effect of the form is assisted by the contrast. In decorative treatments this is almost the same as underlining a word when you are writing.

The example illustrated has the curve of the brow picked out with a dark contrast. This is continued under the eye, following the cut form, and adds in an immediate way to the visual statement. The lighter-toned shape under the black one makes the contrast slightly more subtle and interesting, and its curled ends effectively mask the edges of the basic shape on which the head is built. Slightly curved shapes at the top of the head also mask out the band which holds the mask in position.

The technique of contrasting simple, added shapes has already been examined in earlier exercises, but you could still gain experience by experimenting both with edge patterns and with the patterned effect of placing one shape over another.

This technique will give a cleaner and crisper effect sometimes than free painting, and has the further advantage that added forms can be cut into thin shapes or points and can be deliberately curled. The curling will add to the thickness of the form in the mask and will assist in making it look quite solid.

When the mask is completed all fixing points inside the mask should be covered with sticky tape, especially any fixtures which are likely to come into contact with the wearer's hair. If fixtures are left uncovered they will almost certainly find a way of catching the hair and causing discomfort to the wearer. In a craft this is bad technique, and the craftsman must make a point of seeing that it cannot happen.

Cat heads are required in a number of well-known plays in which some of the characters have to play the part of cats. They can be sufficiently strong if they are made like the ones in this exercise, and can be made visually suitable for any production. For theatrical effect it is useful to aim at getting one very striking colour somewhere in the mask, so that under stage lighting, and against the whole picture of the scene, the mask will have its own particularly striking quality. A black cat, for example, which has a predominantly black mask might have an area of bright blue immediately under the eyes and down the sides of the nose. This blue should be strong and even daring and it will probably be best left in only one part of the mask, so that any effect it makes is not thinned down by being repeated somewhere else.

You will have to look for ways of making effects as you experiment with your masks, but in each one you should try to introduce a note of something simple and exciting — especially if you are making masks for plays. This can be an exciting and interesting part of your work, and besides being useful in the play, anything you succeed in doing should give you a personal pleasure and satisfaction. If it is effective, and you can remember exactly how you achieved the effect, you will add something to your personal skill which may be very useful to you on many occasions in the future.

Dog

At this stage in the exercises you should be beginning to develop an appreciation of the characteristic differences between various head shapes. These might be very subtle, and not easy to see at a first glance, but the experience which you have already had with the flat masks should help you to pick out the important features necessary to a particular head.

A lion is strong in features and is immediately recognisable from the unique mane of hair which surrounds the head. The cat, which is basically very similar in shape,

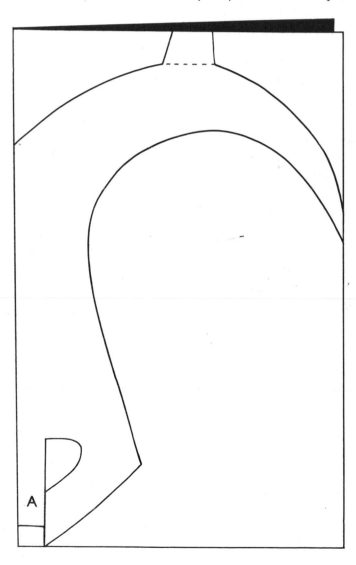

Fig. 50

is less striking in features and has a softer and more subtle general appearance. You have already seen that any shape you attempt must be examined for its particular characteristics, and you will have to continue to do this as you develop further masks into more rounded heads.

In many instances the differences will not be extreme. They will involve the use of a longer or broader nose on the same basic shape, or a longer or differently placed ear. The nose for the cat was different from the lion's, and this difference can be further exploited in this exercise in which the same shape is changed from a cat to a dog.

The nose of the dog (Fig. 50) is basically the same as in previous exercises, but the treatment of the nostrils is again different. Although the change is not very drastic it should make a quite different visual effect to the type of nose produced.

In this instance you should make cuts at the lower end of the nose and a little distance from the centre fold. The cut (Fig. 50 A) should begin at the bottom of the paper, extending a small distance up the nose and turning round on itself in a loop. This makes a shape rather like the letter P, and the paper enclosed in the loop of the cut should come away from the main shape.

A small horizontal cut made into the fold near the bottom of the paper will remove a small piece of the original shape on both sides of the fold. This will prevent the centre portion from sticking down from the open nostril after the shape has been made up.

When the nose is opened out and the nostrils are formed by overlapping (Fig. 51 A) you will have a point of fixture through three thicknesses of paper. The nose will have open nostrils and a blunted end suitable for using on a dog mask.

The technique used to establish this open nostril form can be developed with a number of heads, and is merely an improved version of the simple overlapping technique which establishes form. It is not necessary to worry, in the early stages of considering this variation of technique, whether the three overlapping pieces are exact and correct in measurement, since they can if necessary be trimmed off and made neat after the nose form is raised and fixed. When this nose has been made up it can again be positioned over a simple muzzle form, and fixed with the flaps included at the top. Both the muzzle and the nose must be adjusted and manipulated until they fit neatly on the background shape, and you should not be afraid to alter either of the shapes with your scissors if it is obviously necessary.

After you have satisfactorily fixed the nose and muzzle you can establish the dog more fully by adding the appropriate sort of ears. These can be drooping and spaniel-like (Fig. 51), or they can be variations on the shapes you have already used. The spaniel ears are simple to cut. All you need to do is to fold a large enough piece of paper in two and draw the shapes freely, as large as the paper. After cutting the two shapes together you can fix them at the top of the head on the central band or at the sides of the shape as you have done previously.

The large hanging ears could be edge and surface cut to give more interest to the

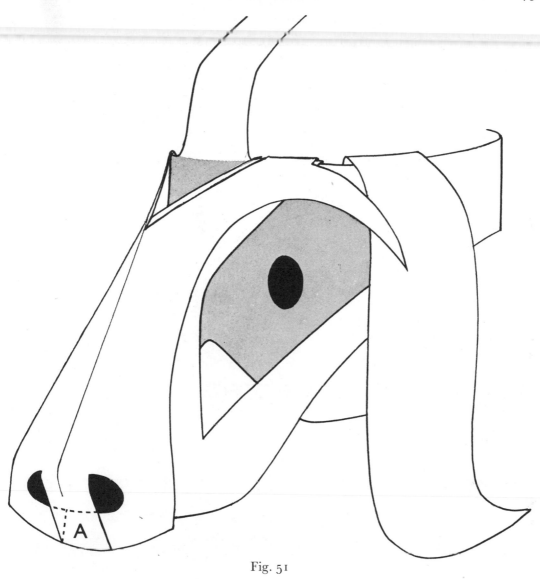

Fig. 51

simple shape. They could also be slightly curled. This is less easy to do with large pieces of paper than it is with thinner strips. It can, however, be done with larger shapes by placing the shape flat on the working surface and holding it against the surface with a ruler or some other straight edge, like a stiff piece of card. If the ruler is held firmly against the paper and the paper is pulled through once or twice in the same direction it should be possible to bend or curl the shape into a pleasing form.

Many dogs are, of course, very hairy and are quite different from the ones illustrated. You should be able, however, to go on from this point, and should be able to

Fig. 52—Simple variations on points like nostrils and ears will help to establish identity and effective difference between masks made in the same way.

introduce any particular sort of characteristic into any dog form you set out to make. You can use the basic techniques illustrated and can exploit them in your own way. If you want a spotted dog you have an excellent opportunity to take the given shape and add your own spots. If you want one of the hairier types of dog with a flatter face you can adjust and trim the shapes until you achieve the effect.

You should be careful at this stage to avoid trying to make your masks too subtle. There are many different breeds of dog, and it would take a very skilled modeller to create the differences between all of them. There is no harm in trying an experiment with a particular breed but you should not allow yourself to become too involved in one shape — unless you have plenty of determination, plenty of patience, plenty of time and a generous supply of paper.

Sheep — Goat

The technique of cutting a nose with nostril openings is further demonstrated in the shape for the goat mask (Fig. 53). This is an advance on the previous example because the shape is designed so that the nostrils follow the line of the nose.

This is another exercise in which you must look closely at the diagram before you attempt to draw and cut it. It is very similar to previous diagrams, but the shape is drawn in a particular way. At its lower end it is tapered towards the centre in a gentle curve.

This curve is repeated above the lower one but in the reverse direction, and is then extended out into the side shape of the cheek. The eyebrow is similar to those used in earlier exercises. At the nostrils the cut is made into the centre fold and then continued parallel to the outer edge until it loops backwards on itself — in the opposite direction from the loop used in the dog's nose.

When the nostril shape is cut the sides can be overlapped and fixed under the lowest point of the central portion. This will raise an interesting form in which the nostrils are oval in shape and suited to the subject. They will occur in the shape over the tapered end of the nose, which will make a curved form for the upper lip (Fig. 55 A).

This is a fairly advanced form and an example of the way in which a definite shape is evolved from the right sort of cutting. This technique is at a stage which requires preliminary planning. It is unlikely to occur successfully in work at this level without preliminary drawing and a searching look, either at the real thing or at photographs and pictures. A successful styling can often be achieved by experiment and pattern making in wrapping paper or in offcuts left over from previous exercises.

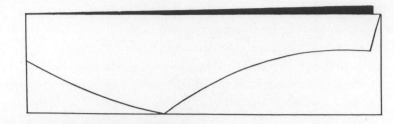

Fig. 54

Fig. 53

A simple lower jaw can be cut for this mask (Fig. 54) and can be fixed to the main
shape in a suitable slightly opened position. Fixing it in an open position is desirable
so that it does not obscure the carefully worked-out line of the upper lip when it is in
place. It can be fixed to the mask under the cheeks (Fig. 55 B).

To make this shape into a goat you will need to cut long ears. These are illustrated
in the diagram and are included in the paper from which the nose shape can be cut.

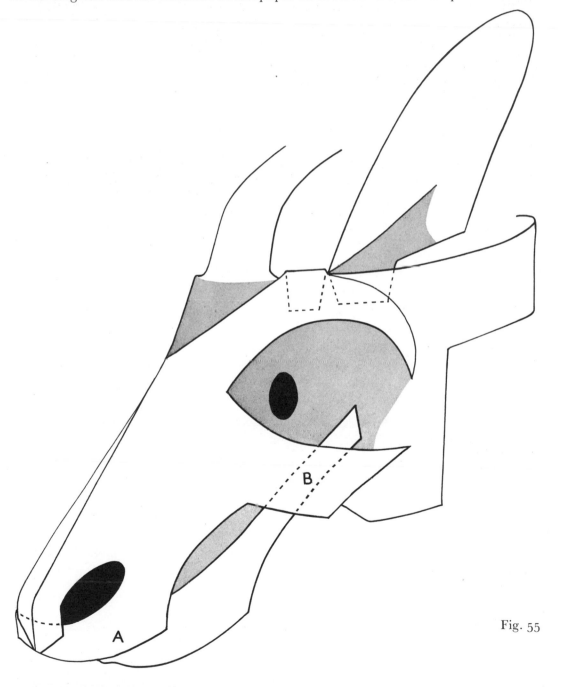

Fig. 55

Fig. 56—The same techniques can be used in many different ways. The nostrils and mouth of the goat are variations on earlier work, with a careful examination of proportion and the placing of parts in the right place.

They are particularly large, and if they are positioned in the right place will add to the line of the mask and will convey a little of the slightly stupid effect which seems right for this animal. For a good visual effect they can be balanced with a curl of whiskers under the chin, and this will turn the shape immediately into a goat. If you want to use the shape as a sheep you must leave the whiskers out and must put lots of curls all over the head. In the illustration (Fig. 56) the more elaborate shape has added horns. These are pieces of paper or card cut into suitable shapes and scored. The score follows the shape of the horn along its length to the tip. The fold raised on this score will give the horns the support they need, and will give them a solid appearance when the light plays on their two surfaces. If the horns are included in the mask, the ears must be placed in the correct position. If you do not know immediately where the ears should be placed you must make the effort to find out, either from a real life visit or from an illustration. As a further simple experiment in this exercise you can try positioning the eyebrow shapes into pleasing curves and fixing them to the mask, either by gumming or stapling. You can also consider the effect of painted or added curls, or any other sort of decoration which suggests itself to you as you work on the shape.

The goats are quite advanced examples of mask-making but they follow exactly the same principles and techniques demonstrated in earlier exercises. Cutting and putting the masks together will not be difficult to anyone who has made an effort to understand the various processes described, and who has developed the ability to look at a diagram and know what it means.

It is also useful when looking at diagrams to be able to see the general differences in proportion between the parts of the shape. If you are able to use a ruler and can measure the diagrams you will be able to scale them up to size to suit the work you are doing. It is not necessary to work with exact and very fine measurements, but it is useful when you are drawing your own diagram to know that you are doing it a certain number of times larger than the printed example.

If you use a ruler as a guide you will also be able to discover the relationship in size between different parts of the diagram you are working on. You will be able to see, for example, that the nose of the goat (Fig. 53) can be cut from a piece of paper which is approximately a quarter as wide again as it is from top to bottom. There are no very definite measurements which you must strictly follow in any of the diagrams, but an ability to see that a certain point is nearer the bottom or almost in the centre will help you in the work. Ears and other additions to the shapes can be cut from the paper left over from the main cuts, as illustrated, or they can be cut with variations in size from paper kept from previous work.

Anyone who has developed skill so far will find it useful to make a simple folder in which to keep offcuts of paper. These need only be kept when they are sufficiently large to be of some potential use in the future, but it is obviously not necessary to throw away every piece of paper which is left over when you have completed any particular exercise. A store of offcuts in various colours and types of paper can be usefully drawn on for whiskers and other decorative additions to your masks. You may not use all the papers you keep, and it might be necessary occasionally to clear out some of your store, but as a general rule it is useful to have a variety of bits and pieces which you can turn to when you are involved in decorating your masks.

If you have attempted this exercise and have successfully produced a goat you should soon be looking for opportunities to branch out on your own. This is not a mask which is particularly intended to test your skill, but it is one which, if completed successfully, will prove that you have reached the point in mask-making where almost anything is possible.

Bear

A technique in the craft is the way in which the tools and materials may be used. A good craftsman usually has considerable technical skill. He knows what can be done with his materials, and is usually able to apply the right sort of technique to the situations which occur as he works in his craft. He is also ready to experiment and explore, and is usually looking for new ways of using and controlling the materials which are available to him.

It is interesting to learn a technique in a craft, and to take it and experiment with it in new ways. This process can lead, like any experiment, to new and exciting discoveries. It is also essential in most activities so that the work does not become mere

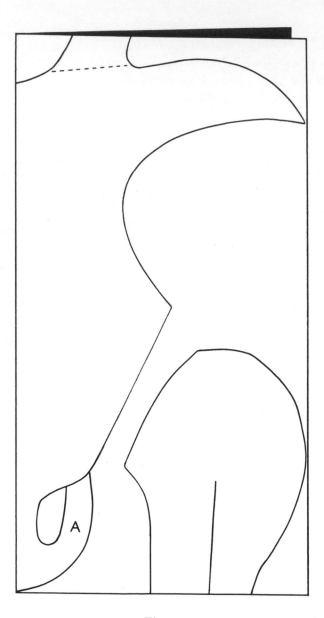

Fig. 57

repetition. Without experiment with his materials and techniques the craftsman who has reached a high standard of work in his craft might maintain the standard, but would be unlikely ever to pass it. The present series of exercises are planned and described in order to give you experience in some of the ways in which techniques can be varied. The most obvious variations on a technique are probably those which involve drastic changes in proportion. An animal mask with a short snout can be made in exactly the same way as one with a long muzzle, but the proportion has to be right to suit the subject. The goat in the previous exercise needs to be fairly long and thin in the nose, but the end of the nose has to be fairly wide. In real life a bear also has a long muzzle but it is rather pointed from the brow to the tip, which ends in a small snout. Techniques which you have been able to practise in earlier exercises should make it possible for you to draw the long muzzle shape. The snout is a shape which will require certain variations on any you have already tried. To make it effectively real it will be necessary, when raising the form at the nostrils, to bend the tip of the nose down and at the same time to keep a particular shape.

The necessary slight variation is suggested in the diagram (Fig. 57) where at (A) a nostril is cut from the outer edge of the nose. If this cut is made as in the diagram, two sides of the nostrils can be bent under the sides of the main shape when it is opened out, and can be fixed in position (Fig. 58 A). The action of bending the sides of the nostrils into position will apply the technique of overlapping in a downwards direction, and you will find that the snout will be formed in the right place.

The thin, pointed shape of the bear's nose must again be supported on a firm foundation, and the simple muzzle shape used in previous exercises can be made to work in this case.

The ears of a bear are a particular shape and must not be cut too large (Fig. 57). They are given form by overlapping on the central cut, and should be fixed to the head at the top of the mask but well to the sides.

For use in a play a mask representing a bear might be given a shaggy treatment all over, as in the illustrated example. This can be done in cut paper or in wool or strips of fabric. For the neatest visual effect the added shapes should be stuck on starting from the bottom and working upwards, so that as in previous exercises the point of fixture is hidden in each case by the next shape above it. The top fixtures which will not be covered can be put on with special care so that your decoration does not end up with an unsightly and untidy final piece.

In its final effect this mask should be quite different from the goat in the previous exercise, but it is in fact made up from the same basic shapes. The techniques are the same because the basic structures of the head are very similar. It is the variations which you can apply within these techniques which will allow you to establish the difference between any characters you set out to create.

The variations on the technique of making the nostril shape have already been described. It you have looked at the diagram (Fig. 57), you will have seen how variations are introduced into other techniques. The eyebrow shape is drawn in a flatter curve for the bear, in order to keep the brow suitably narrow. And since the general nose shape is kept thin, the extensions which are normally fixed at the cheeks are left out. They are not necessary and might, if included, have broadened the narrow shape of the nose.

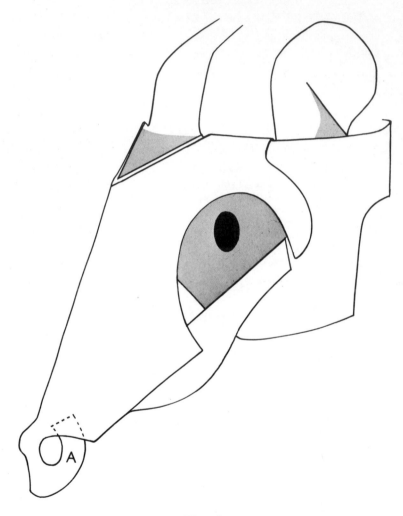

Fig. 58

Fig. 59—A hairy treatment is right for a bear, but the broad brow and narrowing muzzle are important as the right sort of shapes on which to build the decoration.

Fox

In all of the masks which you might have so far made up on a basic shape the support for the main nose has been the same. It might have been necessary to adjust it in size in some instances, but it has not varied in shape from that illustrated in the first exercise (Fig. 41).

For the purpose of the next two exercises a variation will be introduced into this shape. It will serve the same purpose, as a support for the main features, but if it is

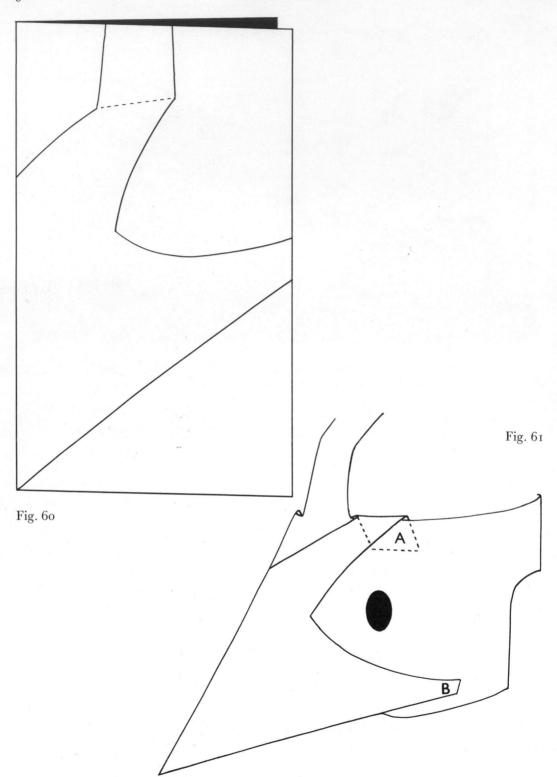

Fig. 60

Fig. 61

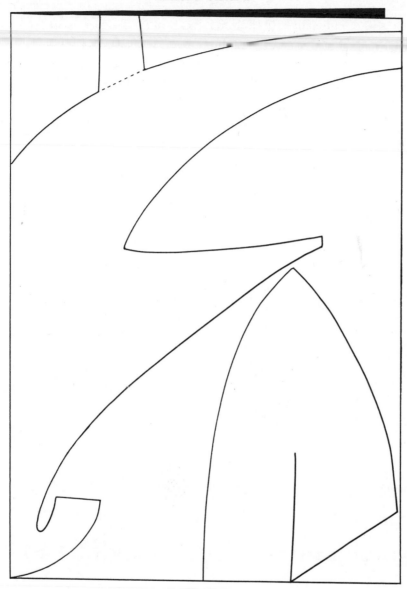

Fig. 62

cut as in the diagram (Fig. 60) it will remain only as a support when it is used, and will not become a visual feature.

The shape illustrated must be cut sharply pointed at the bottom of the fold. It will include flaps at the top for fixing, and pieces at the sides which can be attached at the cheeks.

When this shape is cut it can be fixed to the mask in the usual way (Fig. 61 A and B), and further shapes can be developed on the fixture. The shape illustrated is particularly suitable for masks which must be made up with very long, pointed features.

A suitable development is illustrated in the diagram (Fig. 62), in which the long shape shown can be made up into a fox.

The long shape of the nose is very pointed. It is fairly wide under the eyebrows but is very thin at its end, and includes a simple nostril shape, using the same technique as the one described for the bear in the previous exercise.

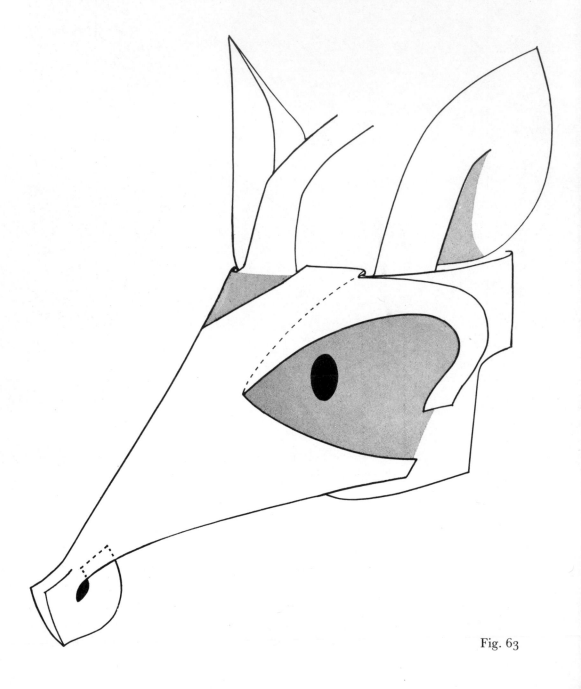

Fig. 63

Fig. 64—An extra large eyebrow fixed at the sides of the mask helps to establish the slinky look essential to the fox.

The eyebrow shapes are drawn deliberately large so that when the shape is made up this exaggeration will form a wide forehead with deep eye sockets. This wide form will contrast visually with the much thinner nose, adding to the impact of the shape. The eyes hidden in deep sockets might convey some of the cunning usually associated with the fox.

When you have cut the shapes and are mounting the nose on the muzzle you should position the eyebrows carefully in pleasing curves, and should fix them at the same point on each side of the mask.

Large ears are necessary for this mask, and are again included in the folded paper used for the main features (Fig. 62). These should be sharply pointed, and should be positioned on the mask in a way which makes the fox look sharply aware of what is going on. It would be pointless to position them in a droopy way which detracted from the general sharpness of their effect. A fox is an alert and lively creature, and the ears should be overlapped so that they are firm and able to support themselves. They should also be positioned with care before fixing, so that they can be used with the maximum visual effect.

If you make up a fox mask and come to the point where you are going to decorate it, you might try to find out exactly what a fox looks like. Some of them have a natural colouring of very attractive red-brown tones which might be exciting to mix and use. The colour is not bright red or dirty brown, which is the sort of colour range one can easily find in mixing experiments. It is a rich, warm colour, and when you have discovered ways of mixing it you can use it to decorate your masks with various tones. Once you have discovered how to make the colour it should be possible furthermore to find it again on any occasion in the future when you might like to use it.

Rat

The rat is also a creature with a particularly long nose, and can be cut in this exercise and supported with the new shape described in Fig. 60.

In this exercise the nose shape can be even longer than that used for the fox, and should be rather more exaggerated in general shape. The diagram (Fig. 65) shows the shape drawn very long and thin. For an interesting visual effect it can be cut slightly wider near the tip of the nose, and can taper sharply in from this point to the nostrils. You can see this in the diagram if you look first at the usual eyebrow shape. This is as broad as the paper, and has a flap at the top for fixing to the basic shape. From the bottom of the eyebrow to the nose the shape tapers slightly outwards from the centre fold. When it is about two-thirds of the way down, the shape changes in direction and turns inwards to the centre.

The cut at the nostrils can be easily understood if it is looked at closely. A vertical cut through the bottom edge turns to the right and back on itself as a flattened loop. A second cut, shorter than the first, will remove part of the paper at the bottom corner of the fold. This cut is designed so that the front teeth of the rat will appear

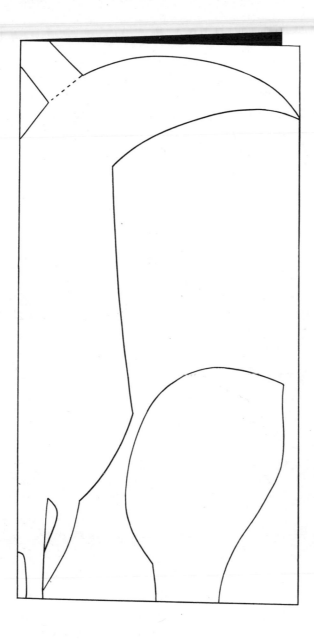

Fig. 65

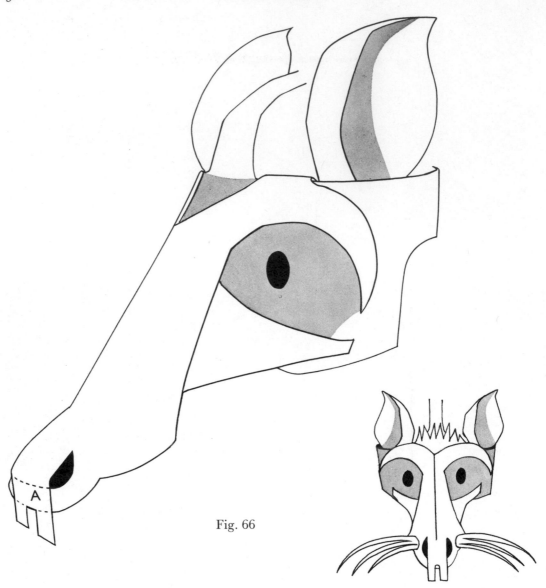

Fig. 66

when you make up the nostril shape (Fig. 66 A). The two teeth can be bent downwards over the two sides of the overlap and can be fixed with the overlaps.

When the nose shape is placed over the supporting muzzle it should be kept as narrow as possible, and the eyebrows should be modelled and fixed with the face suitably thin.

You will notice that the ears for the rat are drawn in the diagram without any indication of a cutting line on which to raise form. In this instance the ears can be cut in one piece and fixed to the mask with part of the front folded back (Fig. 67).

Fig. 67—The ears of the rat are treated differently from previous exercises, and help to keep the narrow form established by the long thin nose.

This is a different but simple way of giving the ears form. It is particularly suitable for the rat, especially if the ears are positioned carefully at the side of the mask. The shape made by folding back the front of the ear is streamlined enough to look right on the thin face, and assists the total visual effect of an animal which is sharp and lean. This is an interesting mask for plays which are either taken from books with familiar characters or for plays which you might like to make up for yourself. If you are making up a play any character might come into it, either human or animal. This is a matter in which you can suit yourself, but some animal identities are obviously more immediately useful than others. This is because, besides being animals, they tend to be associated with a kind of behaviour. A fox, for example, is usually thought of as a crafty or sly character. A sheep is one who is not very bright. A rat, though not very pleasant in real life, might be useful in a play as a rather different character, perhaps one of special importance even.

The masks which you are making at the moment are very suitable for wearing as characters in plays since they do not obstruct the voice in any way and, as you might have discovered, can be used even when the performers who will be wearing them have lines to speak.

If you are using a rat you must give it large whiskers, and must make the character inside the mask brush the whiskers occasionally with his hands when he is performing. This is a typical gesture of many whiskered animals, and is a useful little piece of business which might help establish a character in a play.

The rat might be an important or special character in a play. It can also be a bit of unexpected fun or an amusing character. If you belong to a club or youth organisation and you are at some time preparing a concert, you might consider having a chorus of coloured or spotted rats. It might make an interesting item on the programme, and might add to the pleasure both of the performers and of the audience.

Birds

The pointed muzzle (Fig. 61) used in previous exercises might have suggested a method of making a basic mask shape suitable for development as a bird. The open end at the top of this muzzle, which occurs when the flaps are fixed, is not however really adequate for a beak, since birds do not have a large hole in the middle of the top of their beaks. The shape can be adapted so that the fold of the beak is complete (Fig. 68). In this case the whole length of the fold is retained at the top of the beak.

A flap is included very close to the top of the fold, and the shape is cut with long sides for fixing at the cheeks.

If you look closely at the diagram you will notice that the side of the beak where the flap is, has a very definite curve. This is necessary so that when the beak is fixed the wearer will still be able to see through the holes in the mask. This is the simplest

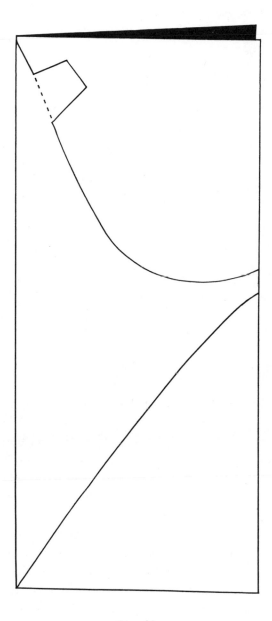

Fig. 68

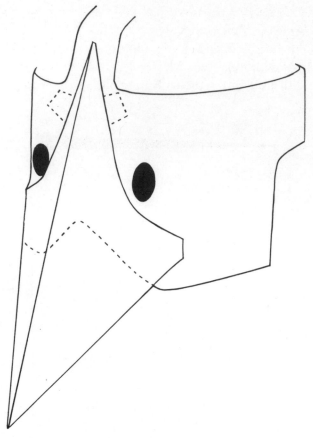

Fig. 69

beak shape for the head of a bird, but it has quite a lot of potential since it can be cut in various sizes. It is easy to fix it to the basic mask by making slots for the two flaps near the top of the basic shape, and by fixing at the sides under the eyes (Fig. 69).

The beak can be livened up with painted decoration and can actually be made to look as though it is growing out of the face of the mask. It can also be made to look like an upper and lower beak in the closed position if lines are painted from the tip to the point where the beak meets the head (Fig. 70).

Like the earlier simpler exercise in bird shapes, interesting plume-like effects can be cut and added, and the masks can again provide excellent opportunities for experiment with attractive pattern and colours. A covering of imitation feathers all over the head could be arranged in the sort of colourful patterns which you can sometimes see on birds. Or you can make up a plumage which has never existed before on any bird. You can make a decoration of feathers which move and sway as the mask

Fig. 70—Birds with a single beak can carry extravagant decoration, and can
be given the appearance of having a double beak if the form is painted with
a line along its length.

Fig. 71

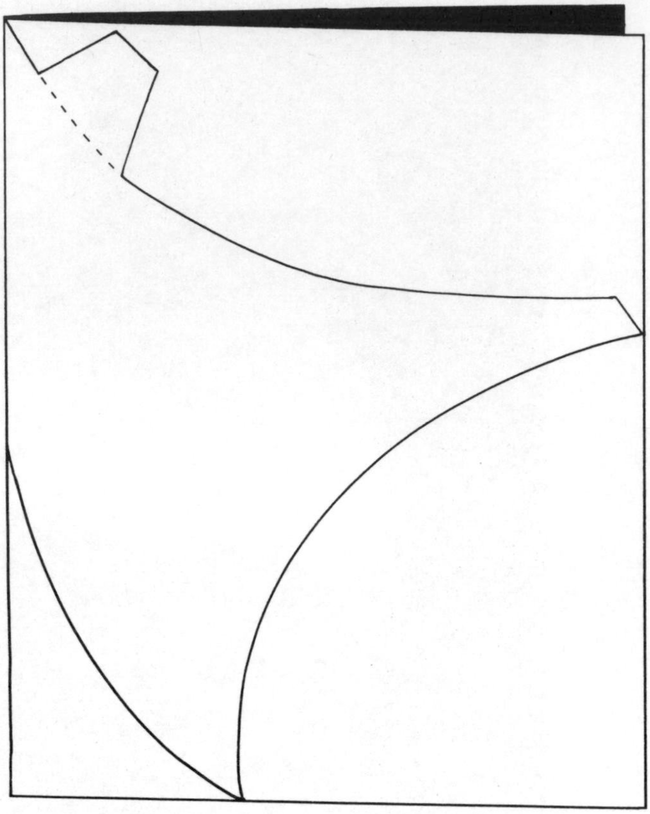

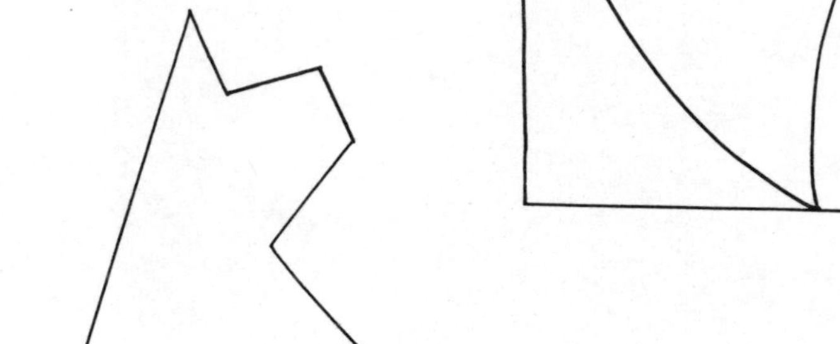

Fig. 72

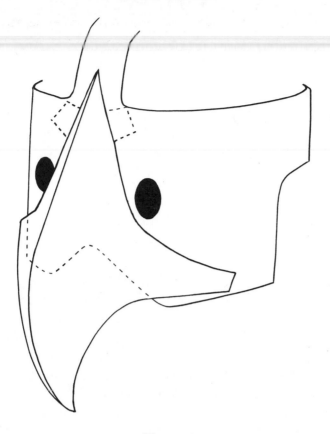

Fig. 73

is worn, or you can make it of good quality paper so that the feathers stand stiff, with perhaps a slight curl at their tips.

The beak shape can be cut in various sizes. It can also be made more varied by cutting it with added curves (Fig. 71). This diagram illustrates a possible construction for a slightly different sort of beak. The lower part of the beak is cut in a curve from the bottom to a point approximately halfway up the fold. Another curve is cut below this from the bottom upwards to the cheek fixture. The curve at the front of the beak will be open after cutting because part of the paper will be removed. The sides of this curve should be gummed together as in the shaded part (Fig. 72), so that no part of the front of the beak is open. The result of this sticking process should be an interesting shape at the front of the beak, which can now be fixed to the mask in the usual way (Fig. 73). This curved shape is a variation on the straight-folded beak since it is not immediately apparent in the mask how the finished effect is obtained. The mask with the curved beak might also seem to some people to be rather more bird-like than the one with the straight fold.

This bird-like quality can be exploited by trimming the rest of the mask to follow the lines of the beak, and by masking the joins with feather shapes or with painted decoration. To be effective the front of the beak must, of course, remain stuck after the beak has been gummed. For best results with any paper or card it is useful to work with a good impact adhesive. If this is used properly the fixture will be immediate and will not be likely to spring open when the shape itself is opened on the main mask. If an impact adhesive is not available and you are going to use gum to make the shape, the beak should be gummed and held together with paper clips until it is satisfactorily dry.

This fixture may be made even firmer with a staple, but staples should not be used when they are large enough to be seen, since this is visually a very important point on the mask.

A further variation on the beak shape is possible by using separate cut pieces for an upper and also for a lower beak. The suggested shape for an upper beak (Fig. 75) is based on shapes used in earlier exercises, and includes fixing flaps at the top of the eyebrows. These are scored for folding and fixing. Enough paper is again included at the sides so that you can make fixtures at the cheeks.

The eyebrow in this instance is given a further variation. It is scored for folding, from the tip through its centre to the point where it joins the main nose. This score is included so that when the mask is made up there is an interesting added visual effect at the eyes. The fold on the score will make the eyes appear to be set in life-like sockets, and it is a technique which can be applied to any mask in which there is an eyebrow shape.

In order that the technique may be fully effective the eyebrow should be cut, at the point where it meets the main shape, from its lower side to the score (Fig. 75 A). This cut will allow the bottom part of the shape to be manipulated so that a clean form can be raised on the scored fold. The positioning of this part of the mask follows the same pattern as previous exercises, and care should be taken to see that it is central on the shape.

The shape for a lower beak can be cut on the fold (Fig. 76) and should be related in size to the upper beak. It is a simple shape without any particular fixing points and, after cutting, it can be opened out and fixed where required to the main mask (Fig. 77). The fixture points of the lower beak can be inside the bottom of the main mask, but you should take care to see that the wearer will not be troubled by a fixture at this point. When you fix the lower beak you must, in fact, watch two points. In the first place it should add to the visual appeal of the mask and should enhance the main beak shape. It should, secondly, be no more difficult to put on and wear the mask with the two beaks than it is with one beak only. The double-beaked mask can

Fig. 74—A curved beak will establish a more bird-like shape than the
simple straight fold.

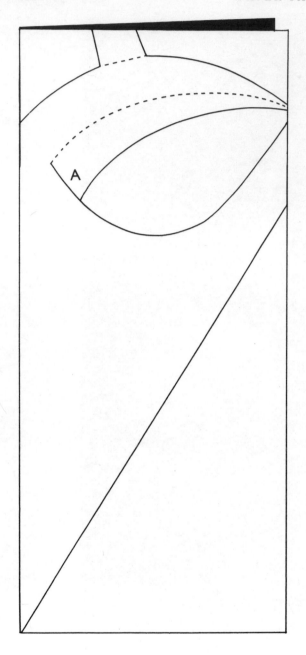

Fig. 75

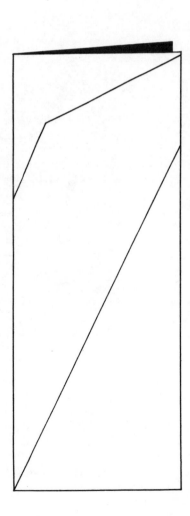

Fig. 76

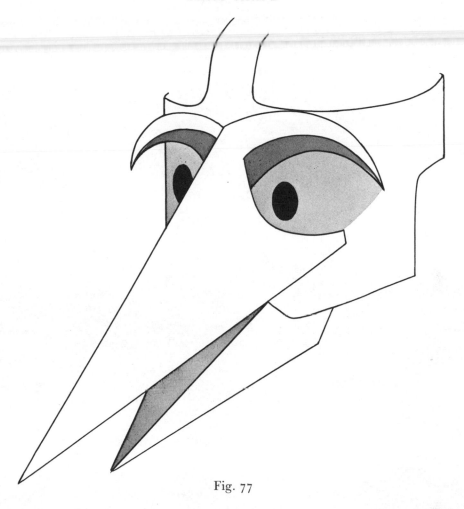

Fig. 77

be very effective when it is made up, and can be quite ambitiously large. If it is going to be made and worn in a play it will be necessary for the wearer to practise and get used to it. It might even be necessary for him to learn to stand in a particular way so that the mask does not really look out of proportion (Fig. 78).

When this mask is made up it will cover the whole face of the wearer but there should still be plenty of space to allow for breathing through the beak. If it is made in thin card the mask will be light in weight, but should be firm and strong enough to carry a large amount of added decoration. If there is the right sort of adjustment and fitting at the back of the head it should be possible for the wearer to learn to move as freely in this mask as in any other, even to the point, if necessary, of running or dancing on the stage.

The range of bird shapes suggested in these and earlier exercises should be large and adaptable enough for almost any purpose. They can be made to wear or they can

Fig. 78—A double beak can be used on the basic shape and will tend to give a bird mask more character than the single straight or curved beaks.

be made as decorative features. If you like birds you might care to see what you can make of them, and you might have the finished heads in your home or school merely as a decoration. You can be almost certain, however, that if you develop an ability to make masks or heads in the shape of birds it will not be long before someone is asking you to produce them for a play or some other special occasion. If you have worked through some of the suggested exercises you should have developed enough skill and technique to be able to do this without any great problems or worries.

Decoratively, birds are some of the best shapes available and you should have fun experimenting with colours and patterns in a variety of different arrangements. The shapes with their beaks are simple and immediately recognisable, and it is unlikely, however wild and free you make your decoration, that you will ever completely lose the visual effect of a bird of some sort.

Donkey — Cow

The technique of scoring and folding the eyebrow shape, which was introduced in the last exercise, can be used in any mask where you want to get extra form into the eyes. When you fold this part of the shape it will take a dark shadow and will give an impression of depth in the modelling.

In all the masks which you have attempted the techniques have been basically the same, and by introducing slight variations of size or actual treatment you will have established different identities in your work. This ability to find different forms is something you will have to look for in the future when you will branch out on your own.

There are almost no limits to the shapes which are possible. Even the most difficult problem will have a solution somewhere. To take a flat piece of paper and make it up so that it looks convincingly like a horse's head might seem an intimidating prospect to anyone who has not had any experience of the techniques already used. But it is really no more difficult to do than any of the earlier exercises in this section.

The diagram (Fig. 79) can be drawn on a piece of paper nearly twice as long as this page and twice as wide. The paper must be of good quality and fairly stiff, and as in previous exercises must be folded longways down the middle. The shape itself is similar to earlier ones and involves the same techniques and treatment. The curved shape at the bottom (Fig. 79 A) is larger than in previous exercises, but when it is cut out it does the same thing. The sides can be overlapped and fixed under the mask in

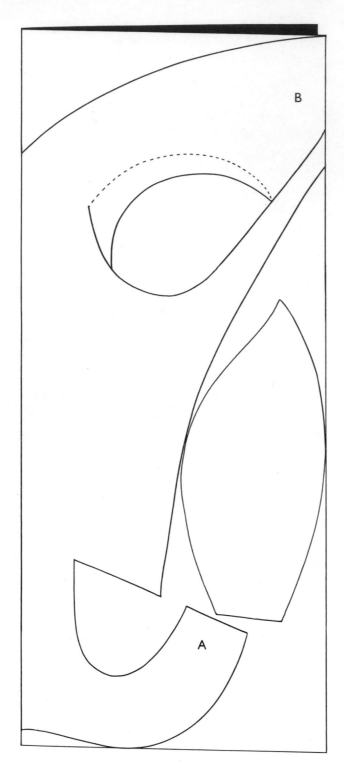

Fig. 79

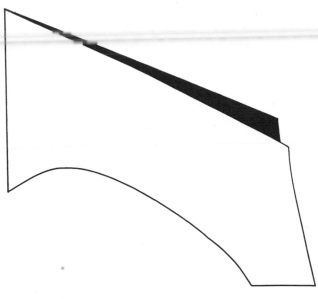

Fig. 80

order to make nostrils. It is designed as a large shape so that when the form is raised in the nostrils the end of the nose will be broad with a heavy-looking snout.

The sides of the top of the head (Fig. 79B) can be fixed direct to the sides of the main mask, and are included without flaps for fixing. The flaps can be left out in this instance, since the fixture will be made well at the sides. You will see from the diagram that a flap could be included at the usual point at the top of the shape, but this is a large shape and it really needs to be pulled out at the sides for support.

The shape itself must obviously be supported on a muzzle as in previous exercises (Fig. 41), and this should be cut to correspond with the main nose. It should be as long as possible without extending below the openings of the nostrils, and it should be firmly fixed to the basic mask before the nose is added.

The fixture for the cheeks is drawn on the diagram below the eyebrow shape, and is made as long as possible. This will give you more scope when you fix the mask at the sides, and will allow you to preserve the elongated look which is suitable for a horse or donkey.

The lower jaw can be a simple shape (Fig. 80) which you can cut from an offcut. It should be shaped with a curve on its lower side, which will give it the right sort of appearance, and can be fixed to the inside of the lower muzzle (Fig. 81 C). If you look at the photograph you will notice how the curve on the bottom of this shape seems to repeat the backward slope of the head, even though it is a very small shape. This is an example of the slight extra touch which you can give to parts of your work for no real reason except that it appears to add something special. It is an individual touch which might be called style, and it is something which will come into your work when you have a real command of the techniques which can be used.

This mask can be made into a horse or a donkey if you vary the size and positioning of the ears. The donkey must have large ears similar to those included in the diagram (Fig. 79). These can be folded in the front as you did in the earlier exercise with a rat, and should be positioned so that they are inclined backwards at an angle, which adds further to the elongated effect which you have already established.

For a horse you will find that smaller and more pointed ears will be adequate.

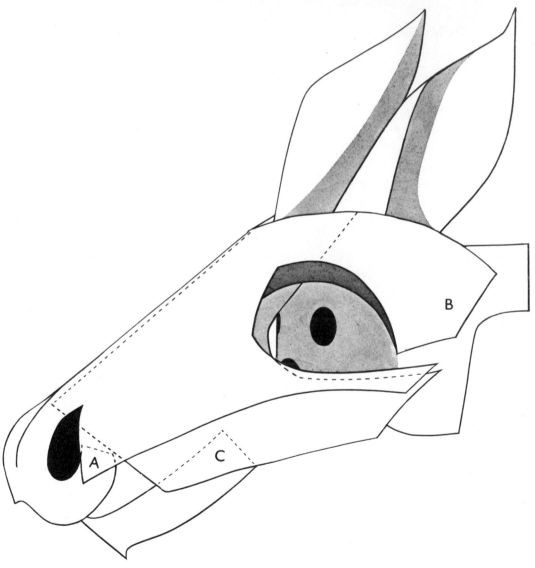

Fig. 81

You can experiment and make these yourself, and can compare the different effects if you are interested.

Trimmings and suitable painted decorations can be used on either a horse or donkey. A little paper, cut as hair and fixed between the ears so that it curls down over the brow, can be particularly effective (Fig. 83).

Large eyes can be painted on the basic shape so that they appear to be in the sockets made by folding the eyebrows.

The shape can be changed easily into a cow (Fig. 82) if you remove the large ears and add simple horns. These should be cut curved and should be scored and folded along the centre. If you are making the shape into a cow you must cut different ears and must place them in the right position outside the horns. If you are not sure about the different positioning of the ears in a cow or donkey you must make a point of looking

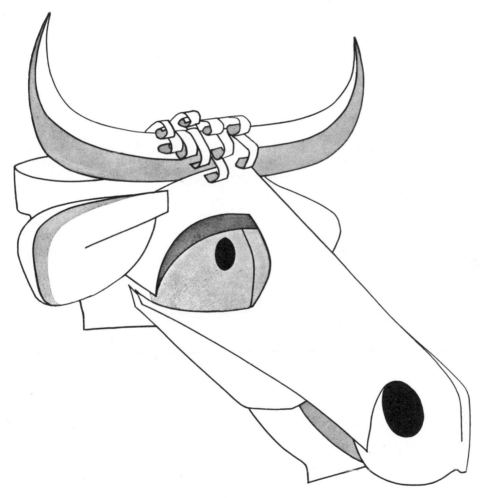

Fig. 82

and finding out. It is surprising how many people will find it difficult to say when asked whether the ears on a cow are outside or between the horns.

This head (Fig. 83) can again be made very large, and can still be expected to support itself as well as any added decoration. You will realise by now, of course, that very thin paper will not be of any use for a mask this shape, and you will realise also before setting out to make the mask that you must have suitable material. If you can get either cartridge paper or thin card you can make this head, and you can make it strong enough for it to be worn in a play or at some other time when dressing-up might be necessary.

Although the mask will be large if you make it as suggested, it should be possible to make it fit quite comfortably by adjustment and careful fitting at the back of the head. You will need help in making this fitting, since it will probably not be possible for you to get your arms and hands in exactly the right position to make the adjustments as you work. But anyone should be able to help if you explain exactly what you need. It should be possible to slip the finished head on and off quite easily. At the same time when it is on it should be quite secure, and must not be fixed with the head bands too loose or it will shift about on your head when you move.

Fig. 83—If the paper is strong enough large masks can be made on the basic shape. These can be planned in the early stages with large features which will convey an immediate visual impact.

Monkey

Most animal shapes can be translated into a fairly simple head by using techniques and methods similar to those suggested in previous exercises. There are a few shapes which are difficult to make up as masks. This is because they are not as easily reduced to simple forms as some of the examples already illustrated.

These shapes are particular animals which do not have the usual forward projecting nose or snout, and they have to be treated individually if the occasion occurs for which they are to be made into masks. It should be possible, however, for you to take the basic shape and to apply the technique you have learned to almost any animal shape.

A monkey has a very distinctive appearance and would be recognised anywhere for what it is, but it is a shape which does not make up easily as a mask. To make a successful mask in the shape of a monkey you will find it necessary to make a different approach to the problem of establishing the features.

You will not find it very profitable to cut and fix a muzzle to the basic shape, and to add a further nose shape afterwards. It will be necessary therefore to approach the problem in a different way, and although you may still use the same techniques, you must be prepared to be flexible and more experimental in the way you use the techniques on some problems.

Monkeys are amusing to watch. They have very expressive faces and are something like humans. But they are not enough like humans to make the simple treatment used in earlier masks effective enough. You cannot make a monkey by adding a nose and hair to the basic mask shape. If you look closely at a monkey you will find that the nose is usually very small, and is really part of a large oval-shaped and projecting jaw.

A gentle oval shape is difficult to establish in paper, but since it is characteristic you will have to accept this difficulty, and then try to overcome it. The answer will be to cut the flat paper with a general oval shape, and to fold it through its centre so that it projects forward. The projection will be in the form of two flat planes instead of a gentle oval, but the outline shape should be distinctive enough to establish the characteristic chin formation. The diagram (Fig. 84) has certain points similar to previous exercises but in some respects it is entirely different. When you read the diagram you will see that it is to be cut in a paper folded at the centre.

In the lower part of the shape a large oval, which is to be the jaw, has a section cut away for the mouth at (D). The side of the jaw is cut with large fixing flaps at the edge (Fig. 84 E).

A cut for the nostrils must be made at the top of the jaw, where the flap for overlapping projects outwards from the top at the edge (A). The portion which is cut away below this flap will form the oval-shaped opening for the nostril. Above the nostril and lower jaw the eyebrow must be made with a steep curve. It should be scored along its length through the middle, and should incorporate a fixing flap at (C).

After you have studied the diagram and understood the instructions, it should be

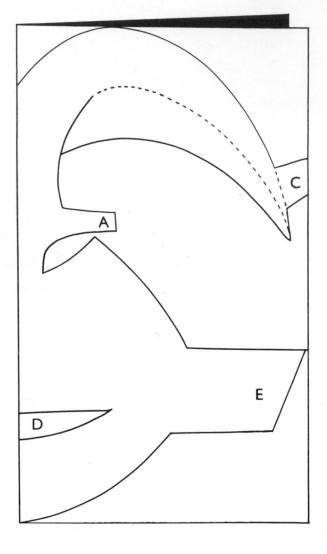

Fig. 84

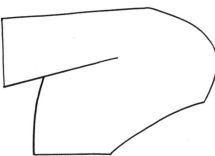

possible to draw the shape on a piece of paper approximately as high as this page. If you can establish the correct height of the shape you will see that the width of the folded paper is almost the same as the height from the bottom of the chin to the nostril. After the shape is cut, the nostrils can be formed by overlapping and fixing the flap at the top of the jaw (Fig. 85 A).

The shape should then be attached to the basic mask at the centre of the nose (Fig. 85 B). This point of fixture is important, and allows you to push the oval shape

Fig. 85

Fig. 86—A hairy or painted monkey can be made as easily as any other mask if the paper is treated in the right way.

of the jaw slightly upwards to form the small nose characteristic of the monkey. When you have formed the nose in a satisfactory position, the jaw can be fixed at the sides of the main shapes with the flaps (Fig. 85 E).

The curve of the brow can be exaggerated by folding the eyebrows along the scores and fixing them in a pleasing shape (Fig. 85 C). You should find that if you push the eyebrows gently towards the centre they will arch and provide the right sort of finishing touch to the rounded form of the nose and curved jaw.

A suitable ear shape is illustrated in Fig. 84. In this instance it is shown separate from the nose so that it does not confuse the diagram in any way. The shape is drawn sideways because the ears should be fixed to the sides of the mask (Fig. 85), and not at the top as in many previous exercises. The ears will again be given form by over-lapping a cut in the middle, and must not be cut too large. After you have cut the parts and have assembled the mask the total effect can be livened up by adding hairy trim-mings. The nose and jaw shape should be left free of any added trimmings, since this part tends to be fairly hairless on the real thing. If you are adding paper trimmings it will probably be best to leave the eyebrows also free, so that they establish a simple smooth curve (Fig. 86). This will contrast with any hairy treatment and should create the right sort of characteristic shape for the monkey.

This is a mask in which you have used the techniques of scoring and of raising form by overlapping. It does not follow the pattern set in previous exercises, but it uses the same techniques in a way which is right for the end product. This is the system you must adopt for yourself for any experimental work in the future. Once you have mastered the techniques it is only necessary to be able to see the characteristic shapes of any animal or human form which you wish to translate into a mask. When you can see and select these shapes you should find your work simple and rewarding.

Frog — Toad

The last shape was a departure from the type of work illustrated in previous exercises, and was an example of the way in which you can master a problem by simplifying it.

Other difficult shapes can be approached in a similar way. You can use the techniques you know in any way you like. The important thing is to make them work for you and do exactly what you want them to. There is no shape which is too difficult. But some shapes will require special treatment because they are so different. If you look at a frog you see something very different from most other animals. Instead of the usual forward projecting nose the frog seems to do something rather similar to

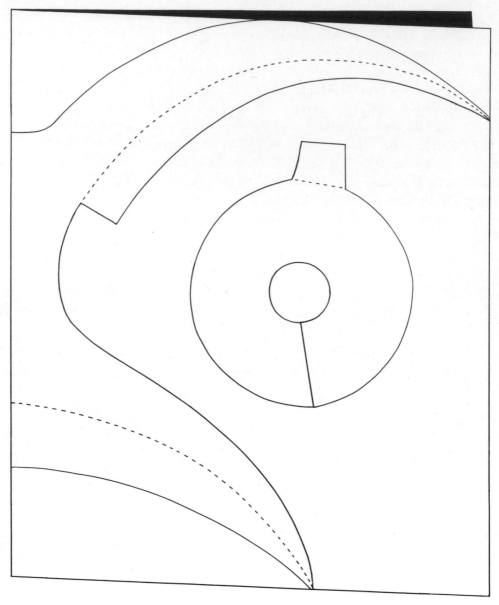

Fig. 87

the monkey. It seems to have an unusually large jaw and mouth, and almost no nose.

To achieve this sort of effect in the previous exercise you took a shape and instead of fixing it at the sides of the basic shape you began by fixing it at the centre (Fig. 85 B). After making this fixture you should have found it possible to push the jaw

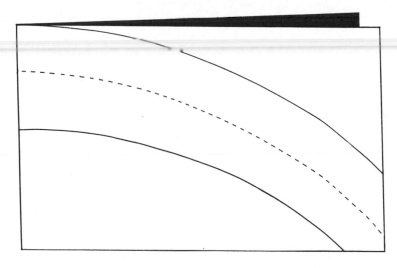

Fig. 88

upwards slightly so that the lower part of the face beneath the nose projected forward. You can apply a similar technique in order to establish the large mouth of a frog. The diagram (Fig. 87) must be drawn on an extra wide piece of paper. You can get some idea of the scale by looking at the illustration of the finished mask (Fig. 91).

The shape is made up mainly of two large curves. The larger one at the top will make a very large eyebrow so that the mask will be very broad-fronted. The lower curve, which is less large, will establish the top lip. In this case it will be a particularly large lip, exaggerating in fact the important mouth feature of the frog.

It should be possible to draw these curves freehand, but if you are uncertain of your ability to make satisfactory curves, you should either use a prepared shape as a guide you can draw round, or you should use a compass. You can work the whole shape out as a pattern on rough paper if you prefer to be very accurate, and when you are finally satisfied with it you can use it folded through the centre and placed on the sheet from which you will cut the mask.

When you have drawn and cut the shape you must open it out flat and must score along the length of both curves from the centre to the tip. The shape must be fixed to the main mask between the eyes (Fig. 89 A), so that you can push the lower part upwards, making it project forward. This forward projection will establish the lip which can be fixed at the sides (Fig. 89 B). The eyebrow shape can be pulled in to this point after folding it on the score, and can be fixed to the main mask.

A simple lower lip can be cut double (Fig. 88) and can be treated in the same way as the upper lip, by scoring it along the length from the centre to the edges. When the

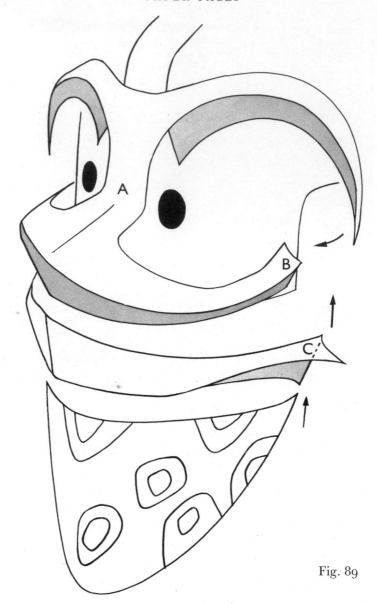

Fig. 89

lower lip is folded into a form it can be fixed to the main mask beneath the upper lip (Fig. 89 C). This should make a large mouth with exaggerated lips.

The total effect of the mask will be assisted if you cut large false eyes from the paper left over from the cut which makes the nose shape (Fig. 87). These should be simple but large circles with flaps for fixing. They can be cut to the centre from the outer edge so that a raised form can be given to the eyes by overlapping the cut. The centre part of the circle should be cut away so that when the form is raised and the eyes are fixed on the mask the part behind the cones can be painted black to give

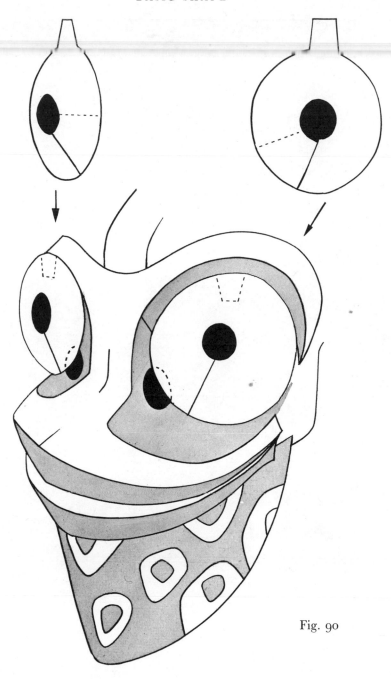

Fig. 90

the effect of a dark pupil in a white eyeball. The artificial eyes in this form can be painted in any way you like, and should be positioned carefully on each side so that they seem to fit with the eyebrows. This is an example of a technique in which the

Fig. 91—The eyes of the mask need not be the ones used by the wearer. Like those included in the frogs they can be large and artificial, the wearer looking through some other part of the mask.

wearer of the mask will not actually use the eyes which are part of the features. The wearer will see through the holes cut for eyes in the normal position (Fig. 91), but this should not be apparent in the finished and decorated mask because the artificial eyes will stand out and command attention. The actual placing of the eyes (Fig. 90) should be done with this in mind, concealing as much as possible of the holes in the basic shape, and at the same time leaving them open enough for the wearer to see through. A simple decorated apron can be fixed at the bottom of the mask to hang down over the chest and complete the frog-like effect.

To make this mask effectively it is necessary to cut the nose and mouth shapes sufficiently large. The rich curves will not be possible if the material is skimped, and it is the curves which give the essential rounded finish to the shape. The false eyes must also be as large as possible, and should almost fill the space between eyebrow and lip. This is a carnival type of mask and it should be decorated in bright colours and simple patterns. It can be decorated effectively in tones of green and yellow, but you should remember to keep the eyes plain, preferably white, so that they stand out against the rest of the shape.

This is a different mask from previous exercises. It is softer in its general effect, and when you put it together you must make sure that you keep the curves uncrumpled. It is not necessary to buckle or crush the paper because the curves are included and cut in the shape and will form the features if you manipulate them in the right way. If you remember this as you work you will respond to the materials and will not end up with something which is so untidy that it has obviously got out of control as you have worked.

DECORATIONS

The range of masks included so far has been concerned with shapes which you might wear. In the text it has been suggested on occasions that a mask which is visually pleasing might be used as a decoration. Most of us like to have things around us which are colourful and exciting, and this applies specially to things which we have made ourselves.

Faces are interesting. Anyone who has worked through some of the exercises in this book should have found himself growing more aware of the faces which he sees every day. He might also have discovered a new interest in looking at the animals and birds which are to be seen either in photographs or in real life.

The fact that faces can be used as a basis for mask-making is obvious. We all of us begin with a mask which gives us an identity. This is the mask which we cannot, of course, change. But we can hide it or disguise it as often and as extravagantly as we like. And we can make and wear masks which represent almost any living or imaginary creature.

Anyone who has decorated masks with colours and patterns might also have realised how effective the faces can be as decorations. There are many occasions when we might want to brighten things up and, for anyone interested, much of the work in this book can be adapted and used in place of bought decorations. Some masks can, in fact, be purposely planned and made as decorations. The three heads (Fig. 92) are made as standing decorations, and are built up on a simple cone shape.

If you take a sheet of paper and raise it to the form of a cone by rolling, it should be possible after fixing the raised form to stand it on a flat surface. If the cone will not stand it can be trimmed at the bottom edge until it does. It can then be used as a basic shape on which to make a face. You have only to add a nose and eyebrows, and perhaps some hair, and when you have painted in the eyes the shape should begin to take on a character of its own.

Any of the shapes which you have made in previous exercises might be simplified and used as a decoration on a cone. Or you can make up new shapes. The Father Christmas in the illustration has a nose and beard shape cut in one on a fold of paper. The moustache, which is cut separately, is fixed into two slots in the beard. If you look closely at the beard shape you will see that the nose is formed by cutting into the centre fold and removing the area of paper which would normally make the cheeks and eyes. With this part cut away it is necessary to paint the eyes on the actual surface of the cone. This is a useful requirement since it will communicate in a simple and effective way a suggestion of form in the features.

A band of paper for the brim of the hat will hide the join between the nose shape and the cone. The tip of the cone can be painted as the hat. This can be done also in the case of the witch, but the hat in this case can be completed by cutting a hole in the centre of a disc and dropping the disc over the point of the cone. The hole must be cut to the size which will allow the brim of the hat to stay in position at the point required.

The features for the witch can be a simple shape with nose and eyebrows cut on a fold. Flaps should be included in the shape so that it can be fixed in the neatest possible way. A score at the eyebrows will raise an interesting form, and a mouth can be cut in any shape which suits the effect you want. A laughing effect can be suggested by having a simple shape which curves upwards. Hair made by using the curling technique is essential to this decoration and, since the intention is not very serious, the curls can

Fig. 92—Faces need not be worn as masks. They can be used as decorations for parties and other occasions, and are easily made on simple shapes.

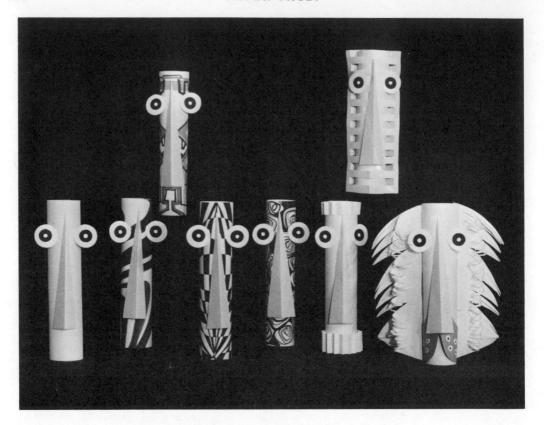

Fig. 93—Many shapes are suitable for development as decorations, and many different treatments can be investigated on the same shape.

be made as luxurious and extravagant as you like. The clown decoration is really a cone on which is fixed one of the simple clown masks introduced in some of the earlier exercises. The hair is an added extra to hide and to exploit the top of the cone, and the eyes are again painted on the surface of the cone. This decoration can be made effectively gay with the addition of a large patterned bow-tie. A number of these in different colours placed at selected points in a room, on the bookcase, a side-table or even on the television will make the room specially attractive for parties.

The cone shape made up as an amusing face can also be useful as a table decoration. For added amusing effect you might put a face on both the front and back of the cone, trying if possible to get different expressions on the same decoration.

The three treatments of the cone which are illustrated (Fig. 92) are intended to be a simple introduction to a possible activity which you might explore more fully in your own way. The cone could be made up as various humans with amusing characteristics, or it might be made up as animal shapes which might surprise as well as amuse your guests. If you are prepared to experiment the cone might be a very profitable basis on which to work both for your own pleasure and for the amusement of your friends.

After working on the cone shape you might examine the possibilities of expanding into other basic shapes. A rectangle of paper can be made up into a simple cylinder which will stand freely without further support. It must be fixed at the back with adhesive tape or with some sort of clip fixture but, after fixing, it can be a useful basic shape on which to develop decorations.

In the illustration (Fig. 93) a simple cylinder is repeated with the same face on it each time. The simple face can be seen in the example on the extreme left of the illustration. It consists of a long nose folded through the centre and slotted into the cylinder. Two simple disc eyes with black rings are also slotted into the cylinder. This combination of three shapes is repeated in each example, and variations are made on the shape with added treatment.

The cylinder can be painted with any sort of decoration. It is really only a rectangle of paper, which is the sort of shape most people are used to painting, but in this case the rectangle is made up and fixed into a permanent cylinder. The painting can be done before the flat shape is curved, and the nose and eyes can be fixed either before or after the shape is made up. A number of these, painted in different colours and patterns, can be placed around the room, or they can be hung with cottons threaded through their tops. If they are made in any size up to about twice the height of this page they will be of very little weight, and the cottons can be pinned to the ceiling or stuck with adhesive tape.

Where there is enough height in the room the shapes can be suspended under each other. If there are enough of them they can be fixed back to back or in groups of three or four and can be hung.

Other treatments in the illustration show the same cylinder decorated with pleated shapes at its top and bottom. In another the cylinder has been inserted into a flat rectangle which has been opened with cut slots. To achieve this effect the rectangle has been folded along its length at the centre and cut through the fold towards the edge at regular intervals with parallel cuts. If none of these cuts touches the outer edge of the rectangle it can be made into a box-like form by opening alternate strips on opposite sides. The visual effect of inserting the cylinder in the rectangle is interesting because of the way the shadows are developed between the folded strips. The nose and eyes can be fixed to the shape after the cylinder has been inserted in the rectangle.

In a final, more complicated, version the cylinder face has been developed into a simple animal head, with a cut and curled mane and an added shape for the mouth. This is an added shape in contrasting colour, and it is fixed with a flap at the top, hidden under the nose, and a fixture at the back.

These various treatments of a cylinder face begin to illustrate a process which could go on through a great deal of experiment. You could investigate how the cylinder would look with drinking straws or with feathers stuck through holes pierced in the shape, or how it would look decorated all over with salvaged scraps of brightly coloured dress material. It might be given a stitched pattern of coloured wool. This could be done easily with a large needle on a cylinder of stiff paper, and you could treat the shape like a piece of embroidered sculpture, building up interesting textures and surface patterns.

There are many possible variations on faces made on a cylinder. And there are still further variations to be investigated on faces made on other shapes. The rectangle of paper which was made into a cylinder could be made into a free-standing triangular or square prism. This can be done by folding the rectangle through its length and raising it to a shape with three or four sides. These shapes could be given a simple nose and eyes and could be used as a basis for experiment with different types of decoration.

There are many types of packaging which can be salvaged and made up into decorative faces. These packages can often be found in interesting shapes. Cardboard drums require only a nose and eyes and suitable pattern in order to convert them from rubbish into attractive decorations. A selection of these, saved over a period of time and then used together, can make an impressive and tall decoration for a party table.

To make these and any other shapes requires two things. In the first place you must be interested, and, secondly, you must have a personal vocabulary of techniques so that when you are about to set out and do something you will be equipped to do it in the right way.

The interest factor is something you must find within yourself. It is the thing which will keep you occupied and will draw you back to the work when you have had to leave it for other things. The techniques are skills which you may have developed through working through some of the exercises in this book.

If you have these two things and a reasonably easy access to materials, there is no limit to what you may do with faces. You can make them up to wear. You can pin them to the walls, hang them from the ceilings or stand them on the furniture. You can surround yourself with your own personal version of the human and animal worlds. You will be able to do these things successfully because you will know how to raise form from flat shapes. You will also know how to select and simplify, and you will be able to make decisions on the most effective treatment to give your faces.

The faces you make will be strange and odd. They will be things you have made yourself as a result of looking at faces and seeing shapes, colours and patterns. The more you look, the more different things you will discover. And the more patterns you make yourself, the more you will appreciate and understand the shapes and patterns and colours which are in the world around us everywhere.

If you use your eyes, and put the shapes and patterns in your own work you will find that the world is an unlimited source of interesting and exciting things to see.

And you will find that the simple business of looking, which is something most of us take for granted, is always worth making an effort over. There are more exciting combinations of colour and shape in this world than any of us can ever hope to see.

You can think of this as you go to a mirror and look at your own face as though you were going to make it up into a mask. After examining yourself closely you should make the mask and should put it on.

As you make the mask you will find out a little about yourself, and you will begin to know what people think when they actually look at you. Afterwards you can pin the mask to a wall and can contemplate just what it is that makes you different from anyone else who has also read this book and is at this moment doing exactly the same as you—wondering what it really is that makes every face so very different from the rest.

FOR TEACHERS

Children like to be actively involved in practical work, and in schools they are being given more and more opportunity to experiment with their hands. This is especially true at the Primary stage where the educational value of lively practical experiment has been totally proved. Any serious theory of education recognises the need for the child to be active and for him to be involved. The materials, tools and equipment for practical work are available to almost every teacher, and most children are allowed the opportunity, and encouraged, to experiment with colours and shapes in a variety of media.

In some schools the experimental factor is as expansive as the teachers and authorities can make it, and the children are allowed great freedom for experiment and discovery. In others the experimental factor is balanced with a more calculated system. In both situations various art and craft activities are introduced and made available as part of the school work. Specialist facilities have their place in the school buildings, and teachers have made great effort to gain a personal experience of the techniques involved in a particular craft.

Some teachers are able to organise and support children's activities in a range of materials from paint and picture-making opportunities, through print-making to three-dimensional work in clay and other responsive materials. There are other teachers who would like to be able to enlarge the scope and range of the practical activities which they are able to offer children, but who are for some reason prevented from going far past the business of picture and pattern making. There are overcrowding factors to consider, limited equipments, the urgent needs of other subjects—and there are teachers who find themselves personally unable to stimulate and support children week after week in the creative process.

These and other difficulties will seemingly always exist, and will probably be discussed regularly in the teacher's life, from the first tutorial during training to the final year of active teaching. In spite of any amount of discussion one factor will remain clear. Every teacher who is involved with children in practical work requires a vocabulary of ideas and equipments just as much as he requires a vocabulary of words. To communicate something clearly and concisely a simple and pertinent vocabulary is required, together with the ability to manipulate the parts of the vocabulary with a reasonable style and fluency. But teachers have to do more than communicate. They know they have to stimulate and promote response, and after starting the various activities which will encourage response from children they have to support and guide the developing processes. A lively and active teacher must turn to as many sources as possible for ideas and for suggestions, and as an individual teacher he will work these out for himself in the teaching context.

The work suggested in this book is a small part of a small point of departure which might be useful to some teachers. A picture or a pattern can be drawn or painted on a rectangle of paper. This is a fact which every teacher knows and uses, but many of them are beginning to realise that the concept of free picture and pattern making on rectangles of paper, although an essential classroom practice, is hardly an adequate basis on which to plan one's growth and development as a teacher.

A more extensive vocabulary of practical opportunity is necessary if the teacher is to grow as well as the child. New crafts and techniques have to be investigated and introduced so that children may explore new creative channels as they find difficulties or setbacks in others.

Any of the exercises suggested in this book, particularly the simpler examples at the beginning, can be used as a new and different vehicle for a child to experiment in colour and pattern. When they are encouraged to paint on rectangles children sometimes get their work pinned to the wall. This work however must usually meet a certain standard before it is selected for display, and we tend sometimes to lose sight of the fact that the act of pattern and picture making is ultimately just as important, if not more so, as the tangible artifact of the end product.

Children paint patterns because they like it, and they must be encouraged to go on painting patterns because they will learn from it. But this will only happen if the practical work is supported in the right way. A pattern based on nothing more than luck or on some sort of vague inspiration may be an excellent and telling exercise. But it might also be a pleasant and repetitive doodle through the colours available. A pattern based, however, on the actual examination of a seen thing, something looked at possibly through a magnifying lens, will involve a process of looking and responding. It is neither passive nor soporific, and teachers are finding more and more that this sort of work is enlarging and enriching the development process of the children they are working with.

There are unlimited visual opportunities for pattern and colour experiment available to teachers who are prepared to investigate and explore the visual world with children. There must also be enormous potential waiting for teachers who are prepared to break away from a concept of practical experiment in pattern and colour which is defined as a rectangle which might be pinned to the wall when it is finished—if it is good enough.

A mask can be one of these further opportunities for experiment in a different way with colour and form. In a classroom every child can make or wear a mask of his own.

This might be only one exercise in a term, but if every child is wearing a mask the necessary involvement factor is established, and a little of the concept of an art which goes on the wall if it is good enough can be undermined.

Any teacher who is interested can look through the work suggested in this book and can select and adapt to suit the teaching situation. The suggested shapes need not be followed closely, but the idea is there—an addition to the vocabulary is stated in one way, and it can be taken and used in any way the teacher wants.

Masks require almost nothing special in the way of materials and equipment. They are fun to make and fun to wear. Paper and paints or crayons, some string and scissors are the only requirements, together with a place to work. This is the lesson preparation which might take an idea from this book to the point where a whole class can be sitting in disguise. The practical opportunities involved can be educationally as valid and rewarding as any act of picture or pattern making in the more normal way. It might also be rather more stimulating and interesting to the children, but this is a matter for experiment in the classroom and only the teacher concerned will be able to evaluate this with any certainty.

It is to those teachers who would be prepared to invite the heads of their schools into their classrooms to see a living aviary of imaginary and exotic birds—in paper faces with bright colours and patterns, and who would accept the situation as a valid part of their teaching vocabulary, that the ideas and suggestions outlined in this book are offered.

If some of the ideas help to make a few lessons in the year lively and memorable because of the response and active involvement of the children, they will have made one of the many small contributions which add together into that important whole—the daily excitement and adventure of school life.